Distinguished Inns
OF NORTH AMERICA

A COLLECTION OF THE FINEST INNS OF

SELECT REGISTRY™

Published by

PANACHE
PANACHE PARTNERS, LLC

1424 Gables Court
Plano, TX 75075
469.246.6060
Fax: 469.246.6062
www.panache.com

Publishers: Brian G. Carabet and John A. Shand

Printed in Malaysia

Distributed by Independent Publishers Group
800.888.4741

PUBLISHER'S DATA

Distinguished Inns of North America

Library of Congress Control Number: 2008920701

ISBN 13: 978-1-933415-42-0
ISBN 10: 1-933415-42-8

First Printing 2008

10 9 8 7 6 5 4 3 2 1

Previous Page: Christmas Farm Inn and Spa, page 98

This Page: The Swag Country Inn, page 198

Panache Partners, LLC, is dedicated to the restoration and conservation
of the environment. Our books are manufactured using paper from mills
certified to derive their products from environmentally managed forests.
We are committed to continued investigation of alternative paper
products and environmentally responsible manufacturing processes to
ensure the preservation of our fragile planet.

Distinguished Inns
OF NORTH AMERICA

A COLLECTION OF THE FINEST INNS OF

SELECT REGISTRY™

Gently roused from slumber by the morning's peeking sunshine the sweet aroma of whipped cream and berry-topped Belgian waffles beckons from the kitchen below—but the impossibly soft linens suggest otherwise.

An array of sumptuous breakfast choices and the zestful aroma of a favorite gourmet coffee ensure an invigorating start to a day full of exciting possibilities. Whether leisurely hours are passed stumbling upon the whimsy and surprise of a historical enclave, exploring the terrain of an unfamiliar region, sampling local cuisine or simply curling up with a page-turner on a sweeping veranda, opportunities for restorative respite abound against the backdrop of any of the 400-plus Select Registry inns.

From the varied and immaculate terrain of California and the Pacific Northwest to the captivating shores of the Atlantic Coast; from arid expanses of the Southwest to charming plains and gently rolling hills of the Midwest; and from the majestic settings in the Great White North to the famous hospitality of the Southeast, North America teems with diverse and wholly delightful Select Registry inns. While the particular cuisine, topography, architectural styles and various attractions surely vary from one region to the next, membership status with Select Registry ensures services and splendor of unmatched quality. Presented among the pages that follow is a sampling of the finest boutique establishments in North America.

Top Left: The Monteagle Inn, page 188

Bottom Left: Buhl Mansion Guesthouse & Spa, page 90

Facing Page: The Lafayette Inn, page 138

Foreword

In the late 1960s, one man had an interesting idea. A travel writer named Norman Simpson drove throughout North America in a paneled station wagon, identifying unique places that offered what he called, "good honest lodging, good honest food, and good honest feeling." Through his pioneering book, *Country Inns and Back Roads*, Simpson introduced a new type of lodging experience to the traveling public—an experience based on quality, hospitality and distinctive styles of lodging properties. Today, the association of independent innkeepers started by Norman Simpson includes more than 400 of the "finest inns, luxury B&Bs, and unique small hotels"—Select Registry: Distinguished Inns of North America. The charming inns featured on the following pages represent a wonderful cross-section of the exceptional level of service and quality that consistently defines a Select Registry inn.

The diversity of styles and locations includes magnificent historic homes updated with popular amenities, as well as exceptional contemporary structures. With the public's increasing interest in cultural authenticity and extraordinary travel destinations, it is noteworthy that the properties represented here often pay homage to their location, whether by offering regional menus or through the romance of the inns' surroundings. Imagine, for example, the delight visitors receive from a room with a view, be it a lake with a tangerine dawn, a charming village street, or a panorama of autumn color. That view—that room—spells out romance, relaxation and peace of mind, and it can be found in distinguished inns from the coast of New England to the valleys of California.

Top Left: Glenlaurel – A Scottish Country Inn, page 122

Bottom Left: Middleton Inn, page 184

Facing Page: El Farolito Bed & Breakfast Inn, page 54

At the heart of these great inns are the innkeepers, owners and their staffs—who lovingly and expertly set the standard for superior hospitality and quality in the industry. For many years, a lit lantern was the symbol of our association, representing the "shining light in hospitality." Personal attention and spectacular service are hallmarks long championed by Select Registry, and unsurpassed hospitality certainly continues to be a defining component of each member inn.

Select Registry works to network its members and to promote its diverse properties with the traveling public. In addition to various online media, branding and co-marketing efforts, millions of Select Registry guidebooks have been printed and distributed by innkeepers throughout North America since 1972. With an extended shelf life these books provide essential information for years to come.

Above: The Hamilton-Turner Inn, page 178

Right: Antrim 1844 Country Inn, page 160

Facing Page: Adair Country Inn and Restaurant, page 82

Distinguished Inns of North America is a striking and informative complement to our guidebook, beautifully displaying the best of what our organization represents. We are thrilled to have helped assemble a representative sampling of the properties that comprise our association. A complete listing of our current membership is included at the end of this book and at www.selectregistry.com.

I hope that you will join millions of travelers who have come to recognize that "traveling the Select Registry way" is the essential route for any discerning inn enthusiast.

Warm regards,

Keith Kehlbeck

Executive Director, Select Registry

Right: The Inn at Cooperstown, page 128

Below: Villa Marco Polo Inn, page 36

Facing Page: Two Meeting Street Inn, page 206

Above: Coombs Inn, page 170

Table of Contents

Above: Old Monterey Inn, page 28

Northwestern U.S. and Canada

Chapter One

Abigail's Hotel

Victoria, British Columbia

Situated in the heart of Victoria, a quaint port town at the southernmost tip of majestic British Columbia, is a picturesque five-star boutique hotel offering the comfort of a family home with convenient access to the capital's attractions. A charming, Tudor-inspired bed-and-breakfast, Abigail's Hotel is neatly tucked into a cul-de-sac, surrounded by English gardens. Up to 46 guests can enjoy snug rooms, homemade breakfasts and a convivial ambience while taking advantage of Victoria's delightfully mild climate—Canada's warmest— various architectural landmarks, eclectic arts scene and variegated landscape.

The hotel's owner, Ellen Cmolik, purchased Abigail's in 2003 after falling in love with the charming town while visiting her son at university. A retired accountant residing in Vancouver, Ellen found that running a bed-and-breakfast would fulfill her mutual desires to work and to regularly visit one of her favorite destinations. Alongside her well-trained staff of 20, all dedicated to providing impeccable service to every guest—each called by name—Ellen welcomes visitors from across the world. Tourists from the likes of England, Italy and Japan are drawn to Abigail's for its cozy, communal atmosphere that provides people the chance to reconnect with themselves, with their spouses and with others.

Couples find the hotel an ideal site for a weekend retreat. While husbands golf, wives take advantage of Abigail's spa treatment room, or the two can also enjoy a couple's massage. Women traveling alone enjoy the security of a friendly environment in which they can comfortably chat with others. Corporate professionals appreciate both the hotel's home-like feel and its proximity to Victoria's commercial hub. Awakened by aromas of freshly baked breads, guests convene in the dining hall for a full complement of breakfast foods as well as engaging conversations. As an added romantic perk, couples can choose to order breakfast in bed.

Top Left: A bottle of champagne is often enjoyed in front of the rooms' personal fireplaces—perfect for celebrating a special occasion.
Photograph by Peter Holst

Second Left: Tasty enough to get anyone out of bed, a wild mushroom omelet with Canadian-back bacon, grilled Roma tomatoes and parsley potatoes is a favorite breakfast of guests.
Photograph by Peter Holst

Bottom Left: Spinach and feta-cheese egg roulade with grilled Roma tomato slices and chicken basil sausage awaits hungry guests.
Photograph by Karen Learmonth

Facing Page: Abigail's Hotel holds an enchanting allure in the dim light of dusk.
Photograph by Peter Holst

In the early evening, guests join one another for drinks and hors d'oeuvres in the library, where they can relax and visit before venturing out to enjoy one of Victoria's gourmet dining establishments.

Named "Best Bed-and-Breakfast" and "Best Boutique Hotel" by Victoria News' "Best of the City," with numerous other glowing reviews, Abigail's Hotel is captivating the senses of many. The enchanting setting makes it an ideal locale for intimate weddings and receptions. Indeed, a Japanese couple flew themselves and their wedding party from Japan to get married at Abigail's, filling all of the hotel's 23 rooms and requiring a translator to communicate with the staff. The hotel's reputation for excellence in amenities and service— pet friendly, Abigail's has designated rooms for guests with pets, offering leashes and crates at the front desk —clearly precedes it, on an international scale. As Victoria's perennial temperate conditions render the destination "always in season," Abigail's Hotel boasts a full house, year-round.

Top Right: The Orchid Room—one of Abigail's Hotel's gorgeous honeymoon suites—features stained glass windows, a vaulted ceiling and a Jacuzzi for two in the bathroom.
Photograph by Marcus Schlüschen

Bottom Right: Abigail's Hotel's quaint, charming Country Rooms feature either a queen-sized or two double beds and a claw-foot tub in the Italian-marble decorated bathroom.
Photograph by Karen Learmonth

Facing Page Top: Luxurious Coach House Rooms feature king-sized four-poster beds, woodburning fireplaces and Jacuzzis in bathrooms decorated with Italian marble.
Photograph by Rob Destrube

Facing Page Bottom: Anyone can feel free to relax by the woodburning fireplace in the library where guests gather for appetizer hour and enjoy a glass of wine.
Photograph by Keith Moffatt

Carter House Inns

Eureka, California

*E*ureka native Mark Carter's inspiration to build the Carter House came when he found the plans for the Murphy House—a San Francisco home destroyed in the great earthquake of 1906—at an antiques shop in 1982. Designed by famed San Francisco firm Newsom Brothers Architecture, whose Carson Mansion in Old Town Eureka had long held particular appeal for Mark, the drawings inspired Mark and Christi to reproduce the design for their own home. When the Carter House was completed in 1982, the Carters decided that the home would better serve the community if they opened its seven rooms to overnight guests. Now comprising three other houses—the 23-room Carter Hotel, the three-room Bell Cottage and a private honeymoon cottage—as well as the nationally renowned Restaurant 301, the Carter House Inns are among Northern California's most exclusive getaway destinations.

Beautiful in their own right, the collection of Victorian houses is set in one of the country's most exquisite locations. From the region's 100-mile stretch of beaches, including the celebrated Black Sand Beach and its majestic Redwood National Park, to its Patrick's Point and Prairie Creek state parks, the setting proves ideal for those desiring communion with nature, endless hikes and walking tours. Eureka, itself, lays claim to a fascinating history. Home of Fort Humboldt, in which General Grant was stationed prior to the Civil War, the town offers numerous museums, shops and sightseeing excursions to fulfill any vacationer's wish.

Perhaps the biggest draw of Carter House Inns is wine. Open to the public, Restaurant 301 boasts a *Wine Spectator* Grand Award-winning wine list, which includes some from Mark's own wineries, Carter Cellars and Envy, as well as many of the world's finest appellations. The seasonal menu consists of gourmet creations made from ingredients fresh-picked from the inns' organic garden, and diners enjoy perfect wine pairings with every delicious dish. For a romantic couples' getaway or a wedding party, a vacation-like business trip or a girls' weekend at the spa, Carter House Inns suit every fancy.

Top Left: Full of charm, the inns are destinations unto themselves.
Photograph by Bob Pottberg

Second Left: The ambience of Restaurant 301 is unforgettable.
Photograph by Bob Pottberg

Third Left: Warmth and comfort permeate the Library Suite.
Photograph by Bob Pottberg

Bottom Left: Suite 304 includes a fireplace, king-sized bed and view of Carson Mansion.
Photograph by Bob Pottberg

Facing Page: Victorian in style, Restaurant 301 and Carter House Inns feature meticulous architectural detailing.
Photograph by Bob Pottberg

Kensington Riverside Inn

Calgary, Alberta

Welcome to the ideal place: where peaceful haven meets city chic. Kensington Riverside Inn is an incomparable urban luxury boutique hotel uniquely situated just across Alberta's picturesque Bow River nestled between the trendy, shop-lined Kensington district and the booming metropolis of Calgary—an unlikely and remarkable juxtaposition. This stylishly intimate inn offers an exclusive home-away-from-home to affluent business travelers, romantic couples and savvy weekend tourists who want worldly comforts, the epitome of customized service and unsurpassed gourmet dining experiences.

The posh contemporary ambience is obvious upon entering the award-winning specialty inn. Creamy white Italian leather chairs beckon relaxation contrasted against the deep blue Bisazza glass-tiled feature wall, Morosini lighting, Ulf Moritz wall coverings and contemporary art all serve to evoke a mood of pure sophistication. While the design elements imbue an air of refinement, the promise of personalized service is underscored when innkeeper Denis Barghshoon and his staff cordially greet guests and escort them to their luxurious private room or fabulous suite. Each of the 19 rooms is meticulously tailored with beds dressed in exquisite Frette linens for a crisp, clean European flair—flat-screen televisions, customized wine fridges, luxury amenities and extraordinary touches exceed guests' expectations. An early morning carafe of freshly brewed coffee with pastry and local newspaper are delivered as a gentle awakening to each guest's day, preceding a gourmet breakfast at Chef's Table on the main floor. Visitors appreciate the generous, attentive service and impeccable style.

The urban-chic Hotel Arts acquired Kensington Riverside Inn, which has consistently been an award-winning travel destination for more than a decade. Not surprisingly, the forward-thinking proprietors have lifted the inn to new heights from its already top-rated status. Previously, acclaimed interior designer Karen Brown took great pride in designing each room to perfection with an inviting French country ambience—today the immaculate inn has been artfully transformed into a refreshing contemporary oasis.

Top Left: The inn's beautiful upscale lounge is inviting day and night—the perfect spot to enjoy a refreshing cocktail or relaxing nightcap.
Photograph by John Bilodeau

Bottom Left: This inn's exquisite evening turndown service welcomes travelers with fine chocolates and the morning breakfast menu before a restful night of rejuvenating sleep.
Photograph by John Bilodeau

Facing Page: Couples truly savor the inn's Romance Suite to rekindle their love in a serenely elegant setting, replete with fragrant rose petals and complimentary champagne.
Photograph by John Bilodeau

The incomparable inn, by its unusual location alone, melds the essence of Calgary's legendary Old West heritage with an unbridled urbanity that now distinguishes the city. Area developer and visionary John Torode has been instrumental in the residential and commercial revitalization of the city and its neighborhoods, recently adding three 40-story condominium towers overlooking the Calgary Stampede grounds where the landmark summer festival takes place.

Known as Canada's energy capital and the gateway to the majestic Canadian Rockies, Calgary's ultra-citified setting is attracting year-round visitors from

Above: A plush armchair beckons guests in the comfort of a private room creating the perfect cozy corner to catch up on some good reading.
Photograph by John Bilodeau

Left: Reservations are recommended for one of Calgary's finest restaurants where a five-course tasting menu with complementary wine pairings is the chef's specialty.
Photograph by John Bilodeau

Canada, the United States and Europe, making it a diverse and culturally rich place in which to work and play. Exercise enthusiasts can enjoy biking and jogging trails just steps from the inn; nearby historic attractions, sport fly-fishing and winter sports are some of the myriad activities travelers are drawn to, not to mention the great shopping, sumptuous dining, incredible art galleries, theaters and music performance venues in and around Calgary.

This designer inn is a rare find in the region and offers business and leisure travelers a remarkable full-service experience. Catering to the individual's every whim with good taste and modern elegance, elite dining is by far the inn's pièce de résistance. In 2008, the management unveiled a new fine-dining restaurant, Chef's Table—since its grand opening, the inn has become a food and wine connoisseur's dream destination. The multi-course tasting menu features regional produce prepared with traditional European methods but contemporized with some new approaches. Full breakfasts include signature dishes such as smoked-salmon eggs Benedict with fresh herb Hollandaise, and dinner cuisine presents regional delicacies of roasted elk and poached arctic char from pristine waters. The art and appreciation of preparing and savoring gourmet cuisine has been perfected and is truly

the inn's calling card. Appealing to all of the senses, this fashionable inn offers a total experience that will long be remembered.

Reasons to visit this superb inn abound. Whether travelers come for a luxury stop on the way to a wine tasting tour in British Columbia, an intimate getaway before boarding the Royal Canadian Pacific for a scenic railway journey through the Rockies or a getaway to Banff Lake Louise Mountain Resort for world-class skiing—Kensington Riverside Inn is the veritable urban escape.

Above: The inn's luxurious suites have glittering views of Calgary to energize the spirit, while the warm fireside setting offers a peaceful haven for pleasant conversation or a revitalizing nap.
Photograph by John Bilodeau

Old Monterey Inn

Monterey, California

From San Francisco, heading south on Highway 1, travelers will go through wooded hills, astride the vast panoramic of the Pacific, through artichoke farmland and finally into sparkling Monterey Bay. Tucked into an acre of gorgeous gardens, amidst the imposing oaks and redwoods of California, lies the ivy-covered Old Monterey Inn. This is a true luxury inn experience.

Even when Patti Valletta was not an innkeeper—no matter where in the world she found herself—she had an innkeeper's perspective. The generosity toward comfort is ingrained. "It's not a nine-to-five job," she says, "it's really a way of life." Everything she is becomes integrated with the inn, and when this comes to fruition, the results are astounding. In fact, her tendency to go overboard has a profound impact on Old Monterey Inn's guests. We should all be so lucky.

Old Monterey is a family of 10—that is to say, the staff members become such under Patti's influence. This encompassing bigheartedness extends to the guests, for the inn's treatment of visitors is a collection of everything Patti has learned, not only during her years as a true innkeeper, but also as a human. This treatment is what really separates Old Monterey from the typical bed-and-breakfast.

Patti knows that most women like nice things, and this is where her overboard tendencies come about—see, for example, the truffles that sit in the rooms, waiting patiently for bags to be unpacked; or, perhaps, the inn's wine hour is a more soothing respite from traveling. Inside each of the inn's 10 rooms, guests will find a great deal of personal attention paid to comfort: high-end, all natural Aveda products, French milled soap and the best quality sheets, along with

Top Left: Guests gather around the living room fireplace each evening for wine and appetizers.
Photograph by Grant Huntington

Second Left: Brighstone Suite offers a romantic, Old World warmth.
Photograph by Tom Rider

Third Left: Sunshine, and a little magic, fills this garden.
Photograph by Grant Huntington

Bottom Left: The Ashford Suite, the original master bedroom of the mansion, has a quiet elegance.
Photograph by Tom Rider

Facing Page: At dusk, the warmth glows from the inside out.
Photograph by Tom Rider

a central refrigerator available to all guests. Patti's world traveling has also been the catalyst for private-use safes in each room.

Breakfast at the inn is always freshly made. Alternating the hot or cold fruit first course, the main course can be either sweet or savory, and the whole may be brought out to the garden on those beautiful California days, or even breakfast-in-bed style. This ability to sequester to private spots, in addition to the drawn back locale, makes the inn the perfect honeymoon or special-occasion point—Monterey in a nutshell. The peninsula is one of the most beautiful spots in California, the city itself boasts a wonderful sprawl of restaurants and historic sites and from the Fisherman's Wharf, whale-watching tours set sail. For golf lovers, Pebble Beach is a short drive, and accenting the peninsula's water adventures, Big Sur is close at hand.

But for Patti, keeping the inn good, keeping it sharp, is her vision. Ever since she first set eyes on this three-story Tudor-style manor, Patti knew

that it would be home. People often tell that they heard Old Monterey was wonderful, but that the visit was better than expected. Always promoting additional experiences, striving for the best—this is Old Monterey Inn.

Above: The Garden Cottage window seat offers a wonderful spot to read and gaze out to the garden.
Photograph by Tom Rider

Facing Page Top: Color and flowers and whimsy are the theme of this glorious garden.
Photograph by Grant Huntington

Facing Page Bottom Left: Vine-covered walls add dignity and Old World charm to the entry of this world-class inn.
Photograph by Grant Huntington

Facing Page Bottom Right: The dining room fireplace is one of 14 fireplaces on the property.
Photograph by Grant Huntington

The Shelburne Inn & China Beach Retreat

Seaview, Washington

*O*riginally established in 1896, The Shelburne Inn of Seaview is Washington's oldest continuously operated hotel. The many guests who frequent it can attest that it is certainly among the country's most charming. An architectural blend of Victorian and Craftsman—the latter style the product of a 1911 addition—the inn embodies the romance of an earlier, unhurried era, when an inn was more than a mere temporary lodging place, offering respite for weary travelers by way of a crackling fire, a hearty meal, a home-brewed ale and, above all, warm and friendly innkeepers.

Assuming ownership of the inn in 1977, local artisans and antiques enthusiasts David Campiche and Laurie Anderson have continued and expanded upon the inn's history and traditions. Furnishing each of the inn's 15 guestrooms with beautiful yet practical antiques, the veteran innkeepers have worked to ensure that the atmosphere feels authentic and cozy. Indeed, when they extended and enclosed the front porch as part of the dining room renovation in 1983, they incorporated stained glass windows reclaimed from a church in Morecambe, England. Art Nouveau in style, the windows perfectly meld with the architecture while adding a narrative all their own.

Among The Shelburne Inn's numerous amenities are its incomparable breakfasts, featuring an ever-changing menu of items freshly prepared with ingredients from the inn's garden and the region's native products. The inn houses The Shelburne Pub, which offers an extensive beer selection, including a few locally crafted brews, and the acclaimed Shelburne Restaurant. Serving the finest in regional cuisine inspired by the region's fresh seafood—the Washington coastline produces 20 percent of the nation's oysters as well as an abundance of fish, Dungeness crab and other delectable gifts from the sea—Shelburne Restaurant provides guests convenient fine dining.

Top Left: The combination of authentic period antique furnishings and modern comforts, such as pillow-top mattresses and wireless internet, unites past and present to redefine cozy.
Photograph by Laurie Anderson

Second Left: Light transmitted through stained and leaded glass casts a romantic glow, which suffuses The Shelburne Inn as well as its pub and restaurant.
Photograph by Laurie Anderson

Third Left: Located in mid-town Seaview, The Shelburne's surrounding perennial and kitchen gardens wrap it into a world of its own.
Photograph by Laurie Anderson

Bottom Left: Just a short walk or drive from the inn and retreat, the beach affords sunset views across the Pacific.
Photograph by Laurie Anderson

Facing Page: The Shelburne Inn was established in 1896 and remains the oldest continuously operated hotel in Washington state and is listed on the National Register of Historic Places.
Photograph by Laurie Anderson

Additionally, guests of Shelburne can choose to stay in the nearby China Beach Retreat, a three-room cottage that David and Laurie purchased in 1998 to serve as an intimate bed-and-breakfast. Nestled in a cove in Ilwaco along the Long Beach Peninsula, the circa-1908 home sits on a site once traversed by celebrated explorers Lewis and Clark. In 2006, David and Laurie added a second cottage to accommodate a single couple desiring extra privacy in the serene environment. Known as Audubon Cottage due to the numerous Audubon prints that grace its walls, the bungalow serves as the perfect haven for nature lovers and birdwatchers, alike.

Certainly there is no shortage of activity in the area. With four distinct seasons, the landscape and climate change dramatically throughout the year. During the mild and warmer months, visitors enjoy the region's 29 miles of sandy beach, bird sanctuaries, wildlife refuges and the Discovery Trail, a paved, eight-mile trail that meanders through the dunes from north of Long Beach to Ilwaco, commemorating the bicentennial of the Lewis and Clark Expedition. Long Beach is home to the International Kite Festival, and Laurie conceived and helped launch the area's annual Wild Mushroom

Celebration, featuring cooking classes, mushroom identification classes and wine dinners inspired by rare and savory fungi.

With so many indigenous pleasures to behold, the region faces the risk of exploitation. David and Laurie are working diligently to ensure that its beauty and resources remain uncorrupted. Viewing themselves as the caretakers of both The Shelburne Inn and China Beach Retreat, they strive to create for their successors a lasting legacy of excellent service and many happy memories.

Above: The Audubon Cottage is so named because of the many John James Audubon prints displayed within and for the bird life viewed from its windows.
Photograph by Laurie Anderson

Facing Page Top: Both birds and people find sanctuary at China Beach Retreat, nestled in a cove between the Port of Ilwaco and Cape Disappointment State Park.
Photograph by Laurie Anderson

Facing Page Bottom Left: A goose takes flight at the shore of Bakers Bay, adjacent to China Beach Retreat, near the mouth of the Columbia River, which is subject to tidal fluctuations.
Photograph by Laurie Anderson

Facing Page Bottom Right: Cape Disappointment is one of many stunning vistas that can be savored from China Beach Retreat.
Photograph by Laurie Anderson

Villa Marco Polo Inn

Victoria, British Columbia

*T*he options are limitless: a leisurely game of bocce, a glass of Amarone della Valpolicella Classico, a favorite book while lazing on a chaise lounge soaking up the afternoon sun, the babble of the fountain in an Italian Renaissance garden's reflecting pool or a tranquil sleep in a lavish suite filled with antiques and art. This may sound like the rich offerings of the Mediterranean countryside—Tuscany or Umbria, perhaps. In fact, these features describe the setting at the exotic Villa Marco Polo Inn, set in Victoria, British Columbia's elegant Rockland quarter—just blocks from Craigdarroch Castle and Government House. From explorers to romantics, historians to gourmets, Villa Marco Polo Inn will impress and enchant. One of the region's most sumptuous inns, this classically designed heritage mansion was built in 1923 as a gift to a young bride and is now a magical venue for fairytale weddings and romantic getaways.

Italian by design, Villa Marco Polo keeps true to its well-traveled namesake and features an exquisite collection of Silk Road mementos. The inn's proprietors have spent much time in Italy and the Middle East, and showcase their fascination for these rich cultures by decorating the Inn with Persian rugs, objets d'art, collectibles and décor acquired on their travels.

From the moment guests enter the villa—with its four exquisite suites and generous public spaces filled with antiquities—they will want to take life at a gentler pace. Each room evokes the mystery of far away places: The Tuscan Room displays an exquisite Persian carpet; the formal dining room is lit by an Italian crystal chandelier; and the sun-splashed Orangerie is furnished with tables fashioned of lava rock from Mount Vesuvius. This is a place where time stands still. The architecture and grounds reflect Old World Tuscany with a multi-level garden featuring traditional balustrades, a stone terrace and a reflecting pool. In cooler weather, guests retreat indoors to the wood-paneled library—a cozy space complete with a woodburning fireplace and stocked with books, magazines and board games, as well as an iMac.

Top Left: Elegance and comfort are revealed as the villa's dining room table is set for breakfast.
Photograph by Gary McKinstry

Bottom Left: The living room features an Italian marble fireplace, accented with antiques and Old World objets d'art.
Photograph by Gary McKinstry

Facing Page: A tranquil reflecting pool and a well-manicured garden are the views offered by the Zanzibar Suite.
Photograph by Eliza Livingston

Each spacious bedroom—the Silk Road Suite, the Zanzibar Suite, the Persia Suite and the Alexandria Suite—offers a special charm. Double soaker tubs and separate tiled showers, romantic fireplaces, desks, fine European linens, hardwood floors with Persian carpets and premium king-sized beds are standard. Special touches include the handmade books, classical works of art and antiques from the owner's family collections. With a nod to the 21st century, each suite features pre-loaded iPods and docking stations, wireless internet and private telephones.

Visitors awaken each morning to the aroma of freshly baked breads wafting through the halls. Breakfast is a memorable affair, with four inspired courses changing daily. A fresh fruit plate is followed by warm muffins, such as buttermilk 10-grain or lemon blueberry cornmeal, served with butter and preserves made from island fruits. A savory course comes next, shirred tarragon eggs in crêpe cups perhaps, or zucchini frittatas with pecorino and chives. A sweet finale rounds off the meal, tempting guests to treats such as caramelized pineapple pecan cakes or piping hot lemon lavender soufflés. Ingredients are locally sourced, organic whenever possible and of the freshest quality imaginable.

The staff provides excellent concierge services, guiding guests to take advantage of the island's bounty. This includes local vineyard tours, whale watching, biking trails, inter-island kayaking and the Royal British Columbia Museum, which houses a permanent exhibit of indigenous cultural history.

Perched on the southernmost tip of Vancouver Island, the inn offers quiet privacy as well as easy access to downtown and the inner harbor. Victoria can be reached in 30 minutes by air from either Vancouver, British Columbia or Seattle and in 90 minutes by ferry from Port Angeles or Vancouver.

This five-star Canada Select Inn was the first Victoria property to be endorsed by Condé Nast Johansens.

Above: Evening's twilight accents the lush garden and soothing south façade of the inn.
Photograph by Gary McKinstry

Facing Page Top: The Alexandria Suite with an adjoining sitting room is a popular pick for honeymooners and travelers alike.
Photograph by Gary McKinstry

Facing Page Bottom: With a double soaker tub, guests of the Zanzibar Suite may never leave the bathing room.
Photograph by Gary McKinstry

Washington Square Inn

San Francisco, California

Throughout American history, San Francisco, with its steep, thrilling hills and beautiful Bay unmatched by any large city in the country, has fascinated everyone from Italian immigrants to the likes of Jack Kerouac to antiques dealers. Known as a place that celebrates diversity, San Francisco's famed Golden Gate Bridge—which is actually orange hued—stands as a most welcoming symbol to all who visit and live there.

Located within legendary North Beach, also referred to as San Francisco's "heart and soul," Washington Square Inn greets its guests with all the charm and comfort of a small European hotel. In 2004, upon purchasing the hotel first built in the 1850s and rebuilt in 1910 after the 1906 earthquake and city-sweeping fire devastated it, Daniel and Maria Levin realized the weight of their acquisition. They desired to make their historic inn relevant today, yet a careful and thoughtful reflection of its location and era. Since Washington Square Inn had been an inn since 1978, there was much renovating and updating the Levins wanted to accomplish before they would be ready to open their inn. The prospect of welcoming and pampering guests from all walks of life—and countries—guided and inspired their hard work.

A stay at Washington Square Inn includes complimentary wireless internet access, breakfast, afternoon tea, evening hors d'oeuvres and wine, as well as full office services in the lobby and 24-hour concierge. There are 15 luxurious rooms to choose from featuring European antiques, cable, flat-screen televisions, soft robes and private baths. Some rooms have sitting areas in bay windows, while others offer a cozy atmosphere with private fireplaces. Warmth and hospitality fill the atmosphere of the inn where the staff never tires of describing activities and suggesting sights in their varied city.

Top Left: Telegraph Hill overlooks the city's bustling Financial District.
Photograph by Andrew McKinney

Bottom Left: The moon rises majestically behind San Francisco's famed Coit Tower.
Photograph by Andrew McKinney

Facing Page: Evening falls softly on Washington Square Inn.
Photograph by Andrew McKinney

Ideally situated in the very center of the vibrant North Beach neighborhood, also known as Little Italy, this historic inn boasts beautiful views of Coit Tower, Russian Hill, Washington Square Park and the Cathedral of Saints Peter and Paul. Although North Beach is surrounded by the fast-paced and exciting historic city, it still maintains the easygoing feeling of a village. This colorful and culturally rich neighborhood represents every bit of what makes San Francisco unique: storied cable cars; landmark buildings; extraordinary Bay and city views; an outstanding selection of restaurants, cafes, clubs and saloons with live music and comedy. In addition to North Beach, guests relish touring other noteworthy neighborhoods including Chinatown, Fisherman's Wharf and Nob Hill. Also, one must not miss the opportunity to visit Al Capone's infamous residence for a time: Alcatraz. With so much to do and see in San Francisco, many guests leave the inn with a return visit already in mind.

Above: Each afternoon, guests enjoy a sampling of refreshments in the lobby.
Photograph by Andrew McKinney

Right: Replete with elegant European antiques, the inn's lobby exudes a sense of welcome.
Photograph by Andrew McKinney

Facing Page Top: Room seven, a corner suite, features views of Coit Tower, the park and the cathedral.
Photograph by Andrew McKinney

Facing Page Bottom: Room 16 is delightfully private and overlooks the inner courtyard.
Photograph by Andrew McKinney

Wine Country Inn

St. Helena, California

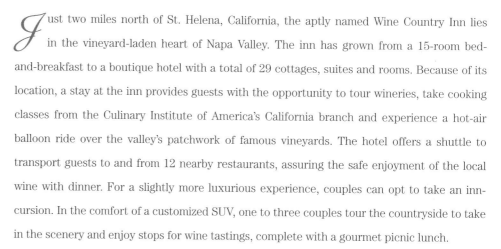

Just two miles north of St. Helena, California, the aptly named Wine Country Inn lies in the vineyard-laden heart of Napa Valley. The inn has grown from a 15-room bed-and-breakfast to a boutique hotel with a total of 29 cottages, suites and rooms. Because of its location, a stay at the inn provides guests with the opportunity to tour wineries, take cooking classes from the Culinary Institute of America's California branch and experience a hot-air balloon ride over the valley's patchwork of famous vineyards. The hotel offers a shuttle to transport guests to and from 12 nearby restaurants, assuring the safe enjoyment of the local wine with dinner. For a slightly more luxurious experience, couples can opt to take an inn-cursion. In the comfort of a customized SUV, one to three couples tour the countryside to take in the scenery and enjoy stops for wine tastings, complete with a gourmet picnic lunch.

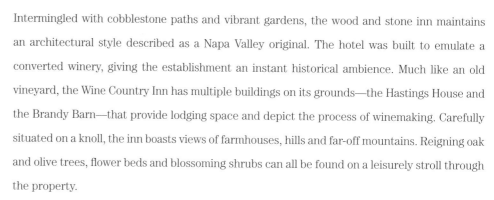

Intermingled with cobblestone paths and vibrant gardens, the wood and stone inn maintains an architectural style described as a Napa Valley original. The hotel was built to emulate a converted winery, giving the establishment an instant historical ambience. Much like an old vineyard, the Wine Country Inn has multiple buildings on its grounds—the Hastings House and the Brandy Barn—that provide lodging space and depict the process of winemaking. Carefully situated on a knoll, the inn boasts views of farmhouses, hills and far-off mountains. Reigning oak and olive trees, flower beds and blossoming shrubs can all be found on a leisurely stroll through the property.

Extensive on-site vegetable gardens yield refreshing juice and produce for the guests. Harvesting tomatoes, sweet and hot peppers, onions and cucumbers from July to November allows the kitchen to incorporate the freshest ingredients into menu items, such as California salsa and hearty frittatas. Along with their breakfast menu, guests may elect to take advantage of the afternoon appetizers—a perfect accompaniment to a bottle of locally produced wine. To further customize a getaway, visitors may choose from packages specifically geared toward their needs.

Top Left: Comfort is an essential ingredient to any stay at the inn. Even if you have a little work to do, the labor will have an element of pleasure.
Photograph by Ed Aiona of Santa Rosa

Bottom Left: A bounty of delicious home-style offerings is the hallmark of both the relaxed breakfast and the stimulating afternoon wine social.
Photograph by Ed Aiona of Santa Rosa

Facing Page: A hand-in-hand, springtime stroll of the grounds at the Wine Country Inn brings the scents of lavender and rosemary.
Photograph by Ed Aiona of Santa Rosa

For instance, there are "men only," "girls' night out" and "elopement" packages. The inn even offers a staff photographer, documenting memories while removing yet another stress for guests.

Since opening its doors in 1975, the inn has been a family affair for the Smiths. Jim Smith, the current innkeeper, is the proud son of the original proprietors and took over the family business in 1982. Each aspect of the inn has been influenced by the family: Jim's father created the original design, his mother decorated the interior, his brother contracted the project and his sister and grandmother crafted quilts and stitched decorations for the rooms. A family atmosphere is encouraged at the inn—relatives serve as housekeepers, managers and maintenance staff members. The family dynamics of the team translate to visitors as a comfortable, pervasive warmth. Thanks to the close-knit personnel, the accommodations feel like an enchanting home away from home.

Top Right: Wine Country Inn welcomes guests in any season. Northern California has a wealth of seasonal variety—visitors can come a hundred times and always be surprised.
Photograph by Ed Aiona of Santa Rosa

Middle Right: Even the pool at the inn has a view to rival any. The relaxing spa services help guests forget to check out.
Photograph by Ed Aiona of Santa Rosa

Bottom Right: With expanses of blue sky and green surroundings, the views can shift a guest's center—making it an ideal vacation.
Photograph by Ed Aiona of Santa Rosa

Facing Page Top: Return guests have a saying, "Once you've gone cottage, you can't go back." With 800 square feet of luxurious, playful space, rejuvenation is almost guaranteed.
Photograph by Ed Aiona of Santa Rosa

Facing Page Bottom Left: Bathrooms are not just for getting clean any more. Guests should plan on an evening in with a simple dinner delivered and a few bubbles in mind.
Photograph by Ed Aiona of Santa Rosa

Facing Page Bottom Right: Even the more standard rooms can be a muse of inspiration.
Photograph by Ed Aiona of Santa Rosa

Above: Inn on Lake Granbury, page 60

Southwestern U.S.

Chapter Two

The Ballard Inn
& Restaurant

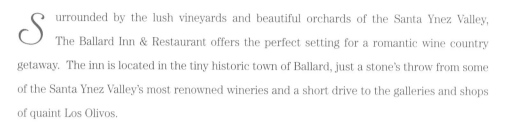

S urrounded by the lush vineyards and beautiful orchards of the Santa Ynez Valley, The Ballard Inn & Restaurant offers the perfect setting for a romantic wine country getaway. The inn is located in the tiny historic town of Ballard, just a stone's throw from some of the Santa Ynez Valley's most renowned wineries and a short drive to the galleries and shops of quaint Los Olivos.

One can't help but relax at The Ballard Inn. The comfortably elegant atmosphere, created with its many roaring fireplaces, inviting seating areas and accommodating staff, puts guests at ease immediately. Each of the guestrooms offers unique decor, some with the rustic and comfortable feeling of a log cabin, others with a more romantic and Victorian feel. Many of the rooms have fireplaces, making for intimate evenings. The Ballard Inn offers guests respite from the hustle and bustle, replete with tranquility. It is no wonder the inn has been voted one of the most romantic inns in the country.

Whether visitors are seeking peaceful relaxation or a more action-packed getaway, there is something for everyone here. Guests can wile away an afternoon on the spacious veranda filled with rocking chairs or rent one of the inn's bikes for a ride along the vineyards and oaks. The inn's on-site wine tasting room features several of the area's best boutique wines and is a great place to start a tour of the area's many wineries.

The Ballard Inn's restaurant, under the direction of chef and proprietor Budi Kazali, is widely regarded as one of the finest in the area. The restaurant's romantic atmosphere, with its warm fire and view of the country, is topped only by Chef Kazali's Asian-inspired French cuisine, sure to please even the most discriminating palates. A dinner here is sure to be memorable.

Top Left: Serenity infuses the inn.
Photograph by Connie Aramaki

Second Left: Iced tea can be peacefully enjoyed on the veranda.
Photograph by Gregory D. Rose Photography

Third Left: The restaurant's signature pan-seared duck breast is drizzled with sweet potato puree and cherry pinot noir sauce.
Photograph by Connie Aramaki

Bottom Left: Local boutique wines are available at the inn's tasting room.
Photograph by Connie Aramaki

Facing Page: Beautiful gardens surround the inn.
Photograph by Gregory D. Rose Photography

Under the direction of its general manager, Christine Forsyth, and its owners, Chris and Budi Kazali, The Ballard Inn & Restaurant strives to create a one-of-a-kind experience, combining warm and elegant hospitality with world-class cuisine. Keeping the inn low-key and down to earth is one of their highest priorities while consistently providing all the amenities and comforts needed to escape the cares of the day. One guest captured their aim perfectly, saying, "The Ballard Inn makes the real world a hard place to go back to."

Above: The Ballard Inn & Restaurant's crisp white fence, gracious wraparound veranda, charming façade and profusion of windows give it plenty of curb appeal.
Photograph by Russell Abraham Photography

Right: Chef and proprietor Budi Kazali offers one of his delectable dishes.
Photograph by Judit and Corina Schweller

Facing Page Top: The Davy Brown Room has rustic appeal.
Photograph by Gregory D. Rose Photography

Facing Page Bottom: An ambience of warmth and welcome pervades the reception area.
Photograph by Connie Aramaki

El Farolito
Bed & Breakfast Inn

Santa Fe, New Mexico

*L*ocated 7,000 feet above sea level and at the foot of the Sangre de Christo Mountains, Santa Fe is an enchanting destination with a rich heritage unlike any other American city—an elevated oasis in the expansive Southwest desert. As the second oldest city in the country, Santa Fe has a deep history comprised of Native American, Spanish and Anglo traditions, all of which are still quite evident today—in the arts, foods, traditional adobe architecture and culture—and make New Mexico's capital a must-visit location for any discerning traveler. For delightfully charming lodging that embodies all of Santa Fe's superb intrinsic qualities within walking distance of downtown attractions, guests need look no further than the El Farolito Bed & Breakfast Inn.

Having already been well traveled throughout Santa Fe and cognizant of its rich character, burgeoning art scene and diverse cultural composition, innkeepers Walt Wyss and Wayne Mainus purchased El Farolito in 1997, seeking a change of pace in a city more on scale with a European city than most American cities. Upon purchasing the inn, Walt and Wayne proceeded to carry out a top-to-bottom makeover that included new furniture, landscaping, art and lighting, among other improvements. These efforts were lauded soon after in 1999, when El Farolito was named "Best Small Property of the Year" by the New Mexico Lodging Association.

Comprised of five distinct pueblo-style buildings, El Farolito's eight rooms are all appropriately Santa Fe-themed and have separate exterior entrances, engendering the privacy of a hotel with the intimacy of a bed-and-breakfast. The rooms are comprised of native natural materials including tile or brick floors, hand-painted tile baths, stone patios, wood timbers and locally produced accoutrements such as original Southwestern art, hand-crafted furniture and folk crafts. Widely hailed for its prodigious art affinity, Santa Fe—a city of just 75,000 residents— has nearly 300 art galleries and more than a dozen exceptional art museums, including the

Top Left: The warm Western décor of the Delgado Room features a queen-sized bed, kiva fireplace and private walled patio.
Photograph by Jumping Rocks Photography

Second Left: The spacious Galisteo Room with its colorful Native American art and locally hand-crafted furnishings is a great place to relax, whether on the adjoining walled patio or in front of a warm fire in the winter.
Photograph by Jumping Rocks Photography

Bottom Left: Hand-carved furniture and local art used throughout El Farolito highlight the rich cultural history and unique architectural style of Santa Fe.
Photograph by Jumping Rocks Photography

Facing Page: Radiant, flowering crab apple trees in full bloom provide a resplendent setting in front of the inn.
Photograph by Jumping Rocks Photography

Georgia O'Keefe Museum, state-owned museums of Native American and international folk art and the Center for Contemporary Arts, among others. Well acquainted with the local art culture and current gallery exhibits, El Farolito's innkeepers are more than happy to steer art buyers—which comprise a significant portion of Santa Fe tourists—in the right direction to locate pieces from their desired genre.

A healthy and delicious meal starts the day for guests at El Farolito in the form of a hot buffet breakfast featuring locally baked goods, yogurts, cereals, juices, coffee and fresh fruit—not just a mixed-up fruit salad, but individually tailored fruit combinations from 10 to 12 varieties of fresh fruit—providing a complete breakfast in a restaurant-style setting. Indoor and outdoor seating is available, and the outside back patio with its ambient fountain is a favorite morning setting. After eating, guests can walk mere blocks away to the heart of the historic district and its renowned landmarks and attractions. In addition to Santa Fe's enticing destinations, nearby locales afford opportunities for convenient day trips. In fact, Walt has recently created five unique itineraries that take guests to exciting proximate destinations for convenient one-day getaways.

For those unable to book a reservation at El Farolito, the owners have a sister bed-and-breakfast, the Four Kachinas Inn. This is a five-room lodging just a block and a half away. In many ways similar to El Farolito, the Four Kachinas Inn is highly regarded in this competitive Santa Fe market. On the popular travel site TripAdvisor.com, El Farolito and Four Kachinas rank first and second out of nearly 40 Santa Fe inns. One satisfied customer eloquently summated the El Farolito experience: "This is one of those places you hate to recommend because you want to make sure that there is a room available the next time you will be there."

Above: Guests can relax in one of several peaceful patio and garden areas located throughout the traditional Santa Fe-style adobe compound.
Photograph by Jumping Rocks Photography

Facing Page Top Left: Guests will enjoy an ample Southwestern breakfast in the dining room, which has traditional Santa Fe-style architectural touches such as vigas (log beams), corbels, a split-cedar ceiling, saltillo tile flooring and hand-plastered, honey-colored walls.
Photograph by Jumping Rocks Photography

Facing Page Top Right: The Santa Fe Suite with its rich warm tones is a two-room accommodation decorated with northern New Mexico landscape paintings, Navajo weavings and ceramics acquired during the owner's world travels.
Photograph by Jumping Rocks Photography

Facing Page Bottom: The Acequia Madre casita is a freestanding building offering privacy and luxury with its rich fabrics, local art and hand-crafted furniture.
Photograph by Jumping Rocks Photography

Fall Farm,
A Fine Country Inn

Mineola, Texas

For many inns and bed-and-breakfasts across the country, charm and historical character are inherent in the structures themselves; but for one Texas inn, the property's history is especially dear to its owners, one that started with them and is still being "written" today.

Fall Farm was originally built in 1979 as a personal residence for the parents of owner and innkeeper Carol Fall. As the story goes, future husband Mike was so enamored with the home and its grounds that upon learning the property was for sale, he purchased it without hesitation—even before he and Carol were engaged. This fact leads Carol to often quip, "Mike bought the home and I came with it."

Opened in 1994, and formerly called Fall Farm Bed & Breakfast Retreat, the inn was renamed to reflect its true offering of so much more. Located on 10 acres of tranquil "piney" East Texas countryside, Fall Farm encompasses the main house, three cottages and a guesthouse. Lovingly, Carol has designed her inn's harmonious, colorful and well-appointed décor. Aside from pampering her guests, it is something in which she excels and delights. Guests find their stay includes all of the wonderful accoutrements one might expect of a fine inn including spa amenities. Diverse in-room packages from a chocolate-dipped strawberry tray to a packed picnic basket prove that Carol and Mike have thought of everything.

Though many guests find little reason to leave Fall Farm's property, antiquing and visiting the many fabulous wineries that have recently cropped up top the to-do list. Magnificent fishing, golf, galleries and shopping within minutes, as well as Canton's famed First Monday Trade Days give visitors—even native Texans—a taste of what is "truly Texan." A premier East Texas inn, Fall Farm has the diversity to perfectly accommodate guests who simply need to reenergize, desire a romantic respite or crave the East Texas experience ripe in Mineola. No matter what motivates guests to seek the beauty of Fall Farm, what they discover remains the same: luxurious accommodations, personal service, warm hospitality and above all, peace.

Top Left: A comfortable, well-appointed Fall Farm suite greets its guests upon entry.
Photograph by Jumping Rocks Photography

Bottom Left: Sissie's Hideaway features a charming and relaxing color scheme.
Photograph by Jumping Rocks Photography

Facing Page: A serene and picturesque atmosphere surrounds Fall Farm at breakfast time.
Photograph by Jumping Rocks Photography

Inn on Lake Granbury

Granbury, Texas

*I*n bright contrast to its rugged frontier beginnings, Granbury, Texas, has evolved today into a graceful, lakefront Victorian town with a bustling tourist business. With a renowned historic downtown square, which includes an 1886 Opera House still in operation, Granbury embodies just the sort of charming country spirit for which the Lone Star State is known.

In 2001, Cathy Casey and Jim Leitch desired a new challenge and change in life, something they could wholeheartedly pursue together. Cathy, a fifth-generation Texan, had regional roots that persuaded the couple to search in Granbury and almost immediately, they set their sights on converting a lakefront property built in 1880 by John Doyle into a fabulous lakefront inn and retreat.

After acquiring the property in 2003, the couple started the immense task of elevating it to an upscale luxury inn and destination. Handsome flagstone was added to the exterior along with interior fireplaces. The couple painstakingly gutted and completely renovated the interior, which now features seven guestrooms with rich, beautiful hardwood floors, maple cabinets and private baths with steam showers and jetted tubs. Well-appointed European décor reflects both casual elegance and Texas flair. The renovation was completed in June 2005.

Guests are extraordinarily pampered—all while enjoying a gourmet breakfast, late afternoon appetizers, lakefront views and a luxury pool with waterfall, surrounded by 200-year-old oak trees and verdant gardens. In addition to accommodating couples' getaways, Inn on Lake Granbury also hosts weddings on the grounds and has state-of-the-art meeting facilities for business meetings and other special events, such as family reunions. With fine dining and entertainment just a short walk to Granbury's historic downtown square, guests are treated to the very best accommodations Granbury has to offer. Hailed by many, including *Condé Nast Traveler* magazine, Inn on Lake Granbury has established itself as one of the most popular inns in Texas.

Top Left: Lounging poolside is a favorite pastime.
Photograph by Jumping Rocks Photography

Second Left: Views of Lake Granbury are savored from the inn's swinging bench.
Photograph by Jumping Rocks Photography

Third Left: The Rio Vista guestroom exudes tranquility.
Photograph by Jumping Rocks Photography

Bottom Left: The Texas Star bathing area is replete with a jetted tub.
Photograph by Jumping Rocks Photography

Facing Page: Dusk falls elegantly on the main house.
Photograph by Jumping Rocks Photography

The Inn on Oak Creek

Sedona, Arizona

*I*n 1996, when Jim Matykiewicz decided to leave Chicago for a rosier real estate investment climate in Arizona, he and his partner, prominent Chicago attorney Tom Stevens, exchanged all of their Chicago-area properties for real estate in Sedona and Flagstaff. By 2005, Jim was looking for something new to do, so they exchanged some of their properties for The Inn on Oak Creek.

Now, Jim is not only the owner but also the innkeeper of The Inn on Oak Creek, managing its 11 rooms with a personal touch. The inn can accommodate up to 24 people, most of whom leave—toothpick in mouth, breadbasket in good spirits—deeply affected by the inn's mouthwatering judgment of cookery. The four-course breakfast wakes guests up with homemade granola and maple yogurt. Fruit, then, is diced and dished—assorted melons or berries devoured lickety-split. Sweet or savory breads follow, and then a hearty entrée—a daily dish interchange of eggs or pancakes and waffles—all brought together by the inn's personal chef. Over the period of a week, breakfast is designed to never be tasted twice. In fact, there is even an opportunity for guests to dabble into the culinary side, as the inn has a chef-taught cooking school, The Art of Cooking, where guests prepare, and subsequently enjoy, a four-course dinner.

Within, the rooms are individually themed. The Bunkhouse is a cowboy's room, with cowboy accoutrements; The Trading Post celebrates American Indians; Hollywood Out West reflects on the old movie industry; all just a sampling of the inn's penchant for the American Identity, and all featuring modern conveniences.

Top Left: Living in luxury, ducks enjoy being fed from guests' private balconies.
Photograph by Jim Matykiewicz

Second Left: Some of the area's best chefs give hands-on cooking classes at the 16-foot island.
Photograph by Jim Matykiewicz

Third Left: Individually designed and decorated rooms like the Garden Gate evoke a feeling of casual elegance.
Photograph by Laurie Dickson

Bottom Left: Each of the luxurious bathing areas—some with red rock views—features a Jacuzzi tub. Warm bubble baths renew mind, body and spirit.
Photograph by Laurie Dickson

Facing Page: Possessing a chameleon-like quality at twilight, the inn's entry leads to a French-inspired country paradise.
Photograph by Laurie Dickson

But The Inn on Oak Creek's setting is its ultimate charm. While green flora is an Arizona rarity, the inn happens to sit on a section of the Oak Creek, which offers such a scarce blossom of color while still incorporating views of Red Rocks, which is just what it sounds like—massive, almost Martian, red rocks. The inn's elevated deck, along with large windows, offers this panoramic as the wide and deep section of the creek straightaway brings out the best in calming fauna: ducks, herons and hummingbirds.

For the inn, creekside is without a doubt the extraordinary architectural feature, surprising even the locals when they wander in the inn's doors for the first time, for streetside could never do justice to the view. As well, a private creekside park functions as a shade supplier for those prone to afternoon yawns and long, reflective moments out of the sun. This is Western comfort at its finest.

Sedona offers many different adventures for the outdoorsy type, including some 130 wilderness trails, hot air ballooning and ancient indigenous ruins, including Montezuma's Castle—a 1,000-year-old, 20-room cliff dwelling—as well as 6,000 years of Arizona rock art; there is even a distinct New Age segment, in the circumstance that a guest would enjoy having his or her aura photographed.

Right: In the evening, the inn appears as another jewel in Sedona's dark, star-studded skies.
Photograph by Laurie Dickson

Facing Page Top: The aroma of fresh coffee greets guests in the scenic dining area, where a mouthwatering four-course breakfast awaits.
Photograph by Laurie Dickson

Facing Page Bottom: Guests make themselves at home in the living room, which exudes French country relaxation with a Southwest flair.
Photograph by Laurie Dickson

The arts community in Sedona is enormous, and The Inn on Oak Creek happens to sit in the middle of the gallery district—Exposures International being the largest gallery in the state. The inn also boasts close proximity—only a few short hours' drive—to the Grand Canyon.

While attracting guests from all over the world, the allure of a three-day weekend brings in its fair share of Californians and Arizonans. A short stint from the 105-degree summer heat of Phoenix down to Sedona's balmy 95 degrees may not seem like much, but it is nevertheless a good excuse to visit the charismatic Inn on Oak Creek. Besides, it is a dry heat, and by autumn, the weather is perfect.

Above: Along with winter comes silence and tranquility; although the leaves are gone, the red rock views are better than ever.
Photograph by Fidencio Soto

Left: At the Trading Post, visitors experience days gone by with the collection of baskets and pots created by American Indians. Red rock views are taken in from the lodgepole bed.
Photograph by Laurie Dickson

Facing Page: Those who stay in Angler's Retreat, the most popular room, awaken to breathtaking panoramas of red rocks and Oak Creek.
Photograph by Laurie Dickson

Martine Inn

Pacific Grove, California

*O*riginally built in 1899 as a palatial home on the Pacific Grove cliffs overlooking the rocky Monterey Bay coastline, Martine Inn had been a private estate for seven decades when purchased by the Martine family in 1972. It was another 12 years before this grand manor finally opened its doors as a resplendent lodge for discerning travelers, but hundreds of satisfied Martine Inn sojourners in the years since would agree that this ethereal stopover in Northern California was well worth the wait.

Fully renovated in 1984, this Victorian home was brought into the modern era with new mechanical and building systems—in addition to ongoing improvements and refinements through the present—while retaining the charm and elegance of a former era. Each room at Martine Inn is reflective of a particular period in American history, replete with priceless American antiques—hand-collected by innkeeper Don Martine over the years—and wallpaper, furnishings and other pieces redolent of a past epoch. Distinct and uniquely configured, some of the themed rooms include: an Art Deco room with Art Deco and Art Nouveau accoutrements from the early 20th century; an Eastlake room with 1870s' Eastlake furnishings; and an early American room with an 1800s' rope bed, Birdseye maple-lined American walnut armoire and 1860 Windsor rocker, among other heirlooms. This exquisite collection of priceless antiques engenders a palpable "living museum" aura throughout Martine Inn, as Don aptly puts it.

The cuisine is fresh daily, served on sets of antique silver and carefully prepared by a head chef with 20 years' tenure. Breakfast includes hot entrées such as the inn's signature dish, Monterey eggs, a delightful fusion of cheddar and cottage cheese with eggs and spices served with salsa and sour cream. Hot and cold hors d'oeuvres are served with wine every evening in the dining room.

Top Left: The filigree slag-glass lamp romantically lights the bedroom.
Photograph by Don Martine

Bottom Left: This private entrance leads to a suite.
Photograph by Don Martine

Facing Page: Located on Ocean View Boulevard, the historic inn boasts a variety of panoramic views of the peaceful Pacific.
Photograph by Todd Hutchings

Martine Inn's compelling environment is second to none. The inn is just a few steps from the water, with a coastal mountain range just 50 miles beyond. Guests can look out the parlor window at breakfast and watch waves crash against the rocks as well as the daily voyages of native pelicans, swimming otters and seals sunbathing on the rocks. After breakfast they can enjoy the 17-mile walking and bicycling path that runs along the coastline.

Though situated in a quiet residential area, the inn is mere blocks away from vibrant local attractions. Popular nearby tourist stops include the Fisherman's Wharf, Cannery Row, Monterey Bay Aquarium, world-class golf courses and more than 40 area wineries, among other enticing destinations. However, many Martine Inn guests fail to leave the engaging splendor of the inn itself.

In addition to its extraordinary natural surroundings, Martine Inn is home to a classic game room, hot tub, 1,000-book library and Don's impeccable vintage car collection. A race car driver for more than 30 years, Don has a one-of-a-kind collection of MG race cars—of which he proudly exhibits six or more in on-site garages—that includes a 1929 MG 18/80 Mk 1 Speed Model sports car—one of only 25 ever made and six currently in existence.

A unique experience filled with daily pleasant surprises in a sublime setting, a stay at Martine Inn is truly one for the ages.

Top Right: Each morning, fresh breakfast treats made with locally grown strawberries are prepared.
Photograph by Don Martine

Bottom Right: Autumn is a beautiful time of year for festivities in the courtyard.
Photograph by Don Martine

Facing Page Top: Mesmerizing ocean views are taken in at twilight from Marie's Room, which is appointed with a variety of fine antiques.
Photograph by Don Martine

Facing Page Bottom: From the Parke Room, guests can either watch in fascination as fishing boats haul in their nets, gaze beyond to the horizon or bask in the lovely interior ambience, defined by the 1860s' Chippendale Revival mahogany furniture.
Photograph by Don Martine

Noble Inns

San Antonio, Texas

*I*f anyone has ever pondered the true definition of "Native Texan," they would need simply to meet Liesl and Don Noble, owners of Noble Inns. Harking back to the days before Texas won its independence, the couple's heritage during the last two centuries reflects their families' active involvement in San Antonio's birth and development. The two can proudly tie several city landmarks and early commercial endeavors to a relative. It is with a history deeply rooted in their beloved San Antonio that the Nobles run Noble Inns: The Ogé House–Inn on the Riverwalk, The Jackson House and Aaron Pancoast Carriage House—each located in the King William Historic District and listed on the National Register of Historic Places.

Begun in the 1850s, the King William area—named for Kaiser Wilhelm I of Prussia and reflective of the area's large German population—became the premier location for the newly affluent to build their residences. Rich with mature vegetation along the famed Riverwalk—that came later—the area has conquered phases that saw environmental catastrophe and its population move to the suburbs, leaving the area to experience an aesthetic downturn. The 1960s saw a renewed interest in the area as people realized the value of the stately old neighborhood and began restoring the homes to their former glory.

Built in 1857, The Ogé House, an Antebellum plantation-style home replete with expansive verandas, was the first significant home in the area. The home was purchased in 1881 by Louis Ogé, who had emigrated from the Alsace region of France in 1845 and made a fortune in the

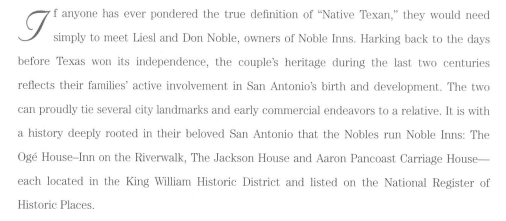

Top Left: Everyone enjoys a delicious breakfast in the elegant dining room at The Ogé House.
Photograph by Jumping Rocks Photography

Second Left: Guests slumber in Victorian charm at a Jackson House guestroom, featuring a double Jacuzzi.
Photograph by Jumping Rocks Photography

Third Left: Furnishings hearken back to an earlier era of elegance and refinement at The Ogé House.
Photograph by Jumping Rocks Photography

Bottom Left: Pampering opportunities are commonly taken advantage of at The Ogé House. Guests can add a special package and indulge in a stay in one of three premier suites.
Photograph by Jumping Rocks Photography

Facing Page: The Ogé House—an Antebellum beauty on the San Antonio Riverwalk—projects a regal presence in the King William Historic District.
Photograph by Jumping Rocks Photography

land and cattle business. He was responsible for adding a third story thereby enlarging the home, while retaining the Greek Revival style. In confirmation of its historical importance, The Ogé House was one of a handful of structures in San Antonio chosen by the U.S. Department of the Interior to be recorded in the Historic American Buildings Survey for its archives in the Library of Congress. While the inn offers 10 magnificent guestrooms scattered on three floors, each one is uniquely designed and filled with many antique furnishings and modern amenities.

The Jackson House, a beautiful Victorian built in 1894 by Moses Jackson, boasts six charming guestrooms on two floors. The home recalls the days of the late Victorian era while providing all the comforts and conveniences

of today, including high-speed internet for the inn's business guests. To guests' great delight, an indoor spa pool is enclosed by gracefully designed, antique English stained glass windows.

Situated behind Liesl and Don's personal residence, across the street from The Ogé House, is Aaron Pancoast Carriage House, built in 1896 by Don Noble's great-grandfather, Aaron Pancoast Jr. Offering a more secluded getaway, the carriage house is nestled under a majestic pecan tree planted in 1900. Three large suite arrangements provide the perfect site for honeymoons, quiet vacations or small reunions. As the parents of three young children themselves who also enjoy staying in distinctive places, Don and Liesl found a void in many up- scale inns and bed-and-breakfasts: More often

than not, they do not allow children. Aaron Pancoast Carriage House presented the perfect venue to remedy that void; suites even include a kitchen. While the other two homes remain adult only to respect the privacy of those taking advantage of a peaceful or romantic interlude, families no longer have to settle for sterile, uncharacteristic lodgings. The three suites can be enjoyed by separate parties or the entire house may be reserved.

Above Left: Visitors at The Jackson House can retreat for a relaxing dip in the heated spa pool after a day of sightseeing.
Photograph by John Dyer

Above Middle: Guests can indulge in secluded relaxation in the suites at Aaron Pancoast Carriage House.
Photograph by Jumping Rocks Photography

Above Right: The privacy of Aaron Pancoast Carriage House offers guests the opportunity to cool off in the swimming pool or enjoy a quiet evening outdoors.
Photograph by Jumping Rocks Photography

Each property distinguishes itself, yet all have in common elegant, well-appointed interiors comprised of American and European antiques, fabulous homemade breakfast and teatime selections, breathtaking views among the gardens and Riverwalk, as well as access to two pools. Concierge service is available seven days a week, assuring that each guest's visit is filled with exactly what he or she had hoped. Romantic and last-minute packages provide a special touch and have been thoughtfully put together. In fact, the couple's classic 1960 Rolls Royce Silver Cloud II is on hand to assure a special journey to anywhere in the city.

Each home is located within walking distance to the convention center, the Alamo, shopping and restaurants along the Riverwalk and in the neighborhood. All are a short drive from several historic missions and sites, theme parks and more.

Top Right: The grand lobby of The Ogé House welcomes guests to a getaway with exceptional service and modern amenities within a stunning historic property.
Photograph by Jumping Rocks Photography

Bottom Right: The elegant Bradbury & Bradbury reproduction wallpaper sets the tone in the entry hall of The Jackson House, presenting guests with a glimpse of the Victorian elegance awaiting them.
Photograph by Jumping Rocks Photography

Villa Royale Inn & Europa Restaurant

Palm Springs, California

*E*ver daydream of living like a 1940s' Hollywood celebrity—jet-setting in California's finest resorts? Reportedly owned by ice skater and starlet Sonja Henie, the 1947-established Villa Royale Inn maintains a timeless appeal that began during Hollywood's heyday. This hacienda-style, Tuscan villa sits in Palm Springs and once attracted the likes of Clark Gable, Cary Grant, Frank Sinatra and Lucille Ball. Two set designers who had worked with Miss Henie purchased the property and added their glamorous stylistic touches to the inn, many of which still remain today. Bambi and David Arnold purchased Villa Royale Inn & Europa Restaurant in 2004 and have made their mark by earning AAA's four-diamond rating and an Award of Excellence from *Wine Spectator*. The inn's hip, long-standing elegance continues to attract models, photographers, authors and singers, and garnered its membership into the Historic Inn Society.

With 30 rooms, guests can choose from individually designed and decorated accommodations, including the villas, royale guestrooms and hideaway guestrooms. Room options include special features like personal patios, fireplaces and even private fountains. Lodgings possess the same quiet tranquility, as the one-story property is set away from major roads and has an inward-facing design with parking on the outside perimeter. These qualities minimize noise and provide visitors with a calm, peaceful environment. The inn is often called "the best kept secret in Palm Springs." Meandering brick paths reveal perfect avenues for casual strolls through the grounds, accented by water fountains, rose gardens and the sweet scent of citrus and jasmine. Mountain views dot the estate, and guests are welcome to take advantage of heated pools and massage sessions in the privacy of their own rooms.

Top Left: Select one- and two-bedroom villas offer a fireplace in the charming living room.
Photograph by Jon Edwards

Bottom Left: Mature trees shade the private patios of a spacious bedroom.
Photograph by Jon Edwards

Facing Page: Surrounded by rooms, the central-courtyard pool is adjacent to the Europa Restaurant and bar.
Photograph by Jon Edwards

Located in Palm Springs, the villa offers both an urban appeal and rustic adventures. Palm Canyon Drive features art galleries, antiques shops, boutiques and night clubs. Here, the International Film Festival draws cinema enthusiasts to screen more than 200 films from around the world. Three Palm Springs museums are in reach of guests, including air, desert and cultural museums. Outdoor adventures abound, with nearby golf courses, tennis courts, American Indian canyons, wilderness parks and desert tours by jeep. For longer excursions, acres of apple orchards lie just one hour from the grounds. A local favorite is the aerial tramway, transporting travelers 8,500 feet to the top of Mt. San Jacinto. The journey affords an impressive bird's-eye view of the desert below and places guests in a dramatically different climate once they reach the desired altitude—temperatures reach as low as zero degrees.

Europa Restaurant has garnered a reputation for fine cuisine with a romantic setting. Upon arrival, guests walk through a charming garden space that leads into an intimate, fire-lit dining room. The menu presents fresh continental cuisine, including dishes like osso bucco—an Italian slow-braised pork entrée—and whitefish grenoblois served in a sweet butter white wine sauce with whipped saffron potatoes. Open in the evenings and featuring a champagne brunch on Mother's Day and Easter Sunday, the restaurant welcomes both guests and local food enthusiasts. Visitors of the inn enjoy a specially prepared breakfast each day of their stay. With years of upscale service, Villa Royale Inn consistently impresses high-profile clientele with both tasteful cuisine and stylish accommodations, perfecting the art of refined hospitality.

Above: All bedrooms are individually decorated with fine linens and antiques.
Photograph by Jon Edwards

Facing Page Top: The lanai is a meeting place for morning coffee and newspapers, while the afternoon welcomes cookies and tea—or perhaps a cocktail.
Photograph by Jon Edwards

Facing Page Bottom: The award-winning Europa Restaurant is open evenings, offering renowned gourmet fare.
Photograph by Jon Edwards

Above: Hydrangea House Inn, page 124

Northeastern U.S.

Chapter Three

Adair Country Inn and Restaurant

Bethlehem, New Hampshire

*D*eliberately small and naturally quiet, Adair Country Inn is rich in history and offers unique New England splendor to all who make its acquaintance. Creating great impressions and lasting memories comes naturally to Adair, where many guests have been warmly welcomed and entertained since 1927. Adair was originally built as a wedding present by renowned Washington, D.C., attorney Frank J. Hogan for his only daughter, Dorothy Adair Guider. The home, expansive grounds and grand gardens are evidence that no expense was spared in Frank Hogan's gift.

Adair remained Dorothy's private residence until 1991 and was converted into a bed-and-breakfast in 1992. It has since evolved into a peaceful and relaxing retreat for adults who enjoy observing wildlife, hiking, golfing, skiing and more in the nearby White Mountains. With its long driveway bordered by stately pines, gleaming birch trees and stone walls, Adair is nestled atop a knoll with spectacular views of the White Mountains. Adair has become one of New England's most renowned Four Diamond bed-and-breakfasts, and has been selected as one of the most romantic inns in the country by American Historic Inns.

The inn's scenic grounds were created by the Olmstead Brothers, whose legendary designs include New York's Central Park, the Biltmore Estate's Azalea Garden in North Carolina and Boston's Emerald Necklace. New England-style stone walls line the gardens, creating secluded sanctuaries that are highlighted by the stillness of ponds and bird baths.

Adair's grounds attract a wide variety of indigenous birds and butterflies. Local wildlife—including deer, moose and bear—can be spotted by lucky guests in the meadows of Adair's

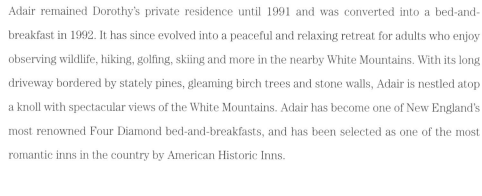

Top Left: Many of Adair's rooms feature spectacular views of breathtaking meadows and mountains.
Photograph by George Mitchell

Second Left: Exquisite fine furnishings, such as this lamp with perforated shade, adorn Adair's rooms.
Photograph by Ed Okie

Bottom Left: Kinsman is one of Adair's most luxurious rooms, featuring a king-sized sleigh bed, Vermont Castings fireplace and magnificent mountain views from the balcony.
Photograph by Tom Bagley/Styling by Gail Greco

Facing Page: Adair's grounds have 200 acres of landscaped gardens and nature trails.
Photograph by George Mitchell

200-acre property. Marked trails guide walkers along natural paths through apple orchards, fields of wildflowers, wetlands and forests of hardwood and pines. The lower gardens are punctuated by wrought iron gates that previously graced the entrance of an embassy in Washington, D.C. Romantic benches are scattered throughout the gardens, creating perfect places for relaxation.

Furnished with many original antiques, the nine guestrooms are each named after a mountain in the nearby Presidential Range and provide a peaceful ambience in which to relax, read or curl up by a warm fire. The natural granite game room is always available for guests' use—playing a game of pool, watching a movie on a large-screen television, working on a puzzle or playing board games in front of a massive stone fireplace.

Breakfast begins with the inn's famous piping hot popovers and fresh fruit and culminates with a delicious hot entrée. Afternoon tea and freshly baked goods are offered for guests' enjoyment upon returning from the day's adventures. For dinner, Adair's restaurant is an intimate and casually elegant environment, with only the freshest ingredients used to produce artfully presented, award-winning food.

For many, the inn is a destination in itself. Adair's innkeepers strive to make each guest feel welcome and comfortable. Amenities include nightly turn-down service, luxurious linens, well-appointed rooms and dinner prepared by an award-winning chef.

Whether a stay at Adair is intended for romance, relaxation or adventure, there is a place and an activity that can be tailored to every guest's wishes. Carefully maintained and thoughtfully managed, Adair consistently pleases the most discerning of guests.

Above Left: Famous wrought iron gates lead to a tranquil country garden.
Photograph by George Mitchell

Above Right: Adair's acclaimed restaurant features delectable dining in a refined, intimate atmosphere. It is open for dinner to guests and the public.
Photograph by Chad Brobst

Facing Page Top: Relax in Adair's cozy granite Tap Room, where the glow from the fireplace accompanies a vintage billiards table, piano, games and large-screen television.
Photograph by George Mitchell

Facing Page Bottom: The spacious Lafayette Room features a cherry four-poster bed, love seat in front of a Vermont Castings fireplace, reading chairs and a view of the front gardens and pond.
Photograph by Ed Okie

Blair Hill Inn

Greenville, Maine

A feeling of awe washes over guests once they have their first glimpse of storied Moosehead Lake with its beautiful bordering mountains—unparalleled scenic views from this exquisite hillside estate are long remembered by those who have visited. The spellbinding allure of inland Maine's Blair Hill Inn is undeniably captivating. An 1891 architectural jewel, the inn is perched upon a 900-foot-long stone wall high above Moosehead Lake, surrounded by seemingly endless views, 15 acres of manicured grounds with vibrant flower gardens and rich woodlands—an idyllic storybook setting beyond one's imagination.

It was an indescribable attraction to the sparkling, crystal blue waters and breathtaking mountain backdrop that won the hearts of Ruth and Dan McLaughlin, owners and innkeepers of this historic specialty hotel. Following a lifelong dream, the couple left the hustle and bustle of corporate careers in Chicago and enthusiastically moved their young family to create a new home for themselves—envisioning their exclusive inn to someday be an internationally renowned destination. The original centerpiece of a 2,000-acre gentleman's farm built by Lyman Blair, a Chicago socialite, the public inn today hosts hundreds of annual visitors from the United States and abroad.

The mansion's interior décor is fresh and uncomplicated. Its great central hall and the grand sweep of the main staircase are an impressive introduction to the inviting beauty found within. To Dan and Ruth, the mark of a successful inn can be likened to a fine work of art that stirs the emotions: "It should touch each guest and make them feel like they have experienced something truly special." Beyond the elegant appointments, the lively spirit of this unique inn is refreshing—it delights the most discriminating guests with an informal atmosphere, yet exudes gracious hospitality—an ambience few places possess.

Top Left: The afternoon sun bathes the inn with a warm glow before setting across Moosehead Lake.
Photograph by Terrell S. Lester

Second Left: Blair Hill Inn has been named one of the five most stunning wedding venues in North America.
Photograph by Russell Caron

Third Left: Ever-present dramatic vistas renew the spirit.
Photograph by Bret Gilliam

Bottom Left: From the high ground of Blair Hill Inn, autumn colors paint the mountainsides as they reach to the shores of the crystal blue lake.
Photograph by Russell Caron

Facing Page: Beautiful gardens bursting with flowers surround the inn from spring to fall.
Photograph by Blake Hendrickson

Eight finely tailored guestrooms are spacious and light-filled—woodburning fireplaces, expansive vistas, fresh breezes and thoughtfully cut bouquets cause people to "fall in love" here. Blair Hill Inn is the perfect retreat for romantic getaways, honeymoons, weddings and reunions, or quiet weekend escapes. Summer concerts are held on the lawn under the stars or inside of the carriage barn—these music performances of classical, jazz and blues are simply magical. Exhilarating outdoor activities abound from mountain hiking, kayaking and fly-fishing to dog sledding, skiing and snowshoeing. Lovely, revitalizing and luxurious, this sunny and spacious inn fosters genuine connections—the innkeepers' relaxed interactions with their guests bring true warmth to the whole experience.

This inn also boasts an exceptional culinary experience. Named as one of the Top Ten Restaurants of Maine, the formal dining room and café porch are renowned for five-course prix fixe dinners prepared by chef Amy Oliver. Her sensibly creative menu, with tempting selections such as pan-seared Maine sea scallops and garlicky tomato-mustard sauce atop fennel risotto or wood-grilled pepper tenderloin in cognac cream sauce with truffle mashed potatoes, pleases the most discriminating palate. The kitchen's woodburning Aztec grill adds a distinctive, earthy flavor to entrées that no other cooking method can achieve and has become the restaurant's hallmark. Accompanied by fine wines, cocktails and apertifs from the inn's full-service bar, an evening of dining is not to be missed.

Dan, an ardent gardener, grows organic herbs, fruits and vegetables that enhance nearly every dish prepared by the professional staff. An equally lavish breakfast, prepared by Dan himself, features a daily gourmet feast. Spicy Maine crab cakes eggs Benedict or custard-like French toast with sautéed bananas and toasted coconut are favorite house specialties.

Top Left: Spacious, bright and elegant guestrooms overlook the lake and mountains.
Photograph by Bret Gilliam

Middle Left: Seven woodburning fireplaces invite guests to relax amidst comfortable refinement.
Photograph by Ruth McLaughlin

Bottom Left: The grand staircase's turn-of-the-century stained glass windows are among the 1891 mansion's celebrated architectural details.
Photograph by Russell Caron

Guests can conveniently fly into either Bangor or Portland International Airport, which are both less than a two-and-a-half-hour drive to the charming village of Greenville. The hospitable inn consistently exceeds expectations and is acclaimed by Christina Tree, famous travel author, as one of New England's most memorable properties. Voted one of the Top Ten Most Romantic Inns of North America for 2007, Blair Hill Inn is a premier destination.

Just as artistic masterpieces are timeless treasures, this quintessential countryside inn is an enduring treasure that brilliantly beckons travelers to return again and again.

Above: A 900-foot stone wall surrounds and elevates Blair Hill Inn to its commanding setting above Moosehead Lake. Hazy days further accentuate the cascading flowers and peacefulness.
Photograph by Lynn Karlin

Right: On the balcony of Blair Hill Inn, morning coffee can be enjoyed while surveying the wilderness landscape that spans from New Hampshire to Canada.
Photograph by Blake Hendrickson

Buhl Mansion Guesthouse & Spa

Sharon, Pennsylvania

*I*t seems poetically fitting that a stunning castle-like home, built by a man for his new bride, should today be the destination for romantic weekends, honeymoons, a reprieve from the stresses of life or even the site of a team-building executive retreat. Poetically fitting as well, in the face of mounting odds, Buhl Mansion triumphed with a "fairy tale ending" of sorts.

After graduating from Yale in the late 1800s, Frank Buhl came to Sharon, Pennsylvania—halfway between Cleveland and Pittsburgh—to join the family business in the steel industry. It was there that Frank fell in love with Julia Forker, and in 1888, they were married. In 1890, construction began on the "castle" Frank's mother insisted he build his bride. By 1896, the Richardsonian Romanesque castle was complete, and it was there they spent their lives as beloved citizens and philanthropists of Sharon.

Frank had remarkable success in the steel industry, and through wonderfully altruistic gestures, the Buhls gifted the community with much, including the area's first hospital, its library, a country club and more. It is said that F. H. Buhl Farm was probably their most generous gift to Sharon's residents. Frank purchased 300 acres of land, dedicating five years to its development, building roads and planting more than 75,000 trees. He built an 11-acre lake—Lake Julia—with a Casino for public recreation as well as a nine-hole golf course. In addition, by the terms of his will, he made necessary arrangements to assure the perpetual maintenance of his projects. Consequently, Sharon has the proud distinction of having the only free golf course in the world, while Mercer County has been counted among the top 10 golf destinations in the country.

Sadly and rather ironically, for all of Frank and Julia's planning and renewing endowments, they left one important landmark's future in question after their deaths: their dearly loved Buhl Mansion. As the two never had children, the home passed hands many times and fell into

Top Left: Castle-for-a-day destination packages promise exclusive use of the mansion and gardens for elegant weddings, social occasions or corporate retreats.
Photograph by Julie Moroco, Moroco Photography

Second Left: Buhl Mansion Spa's romance package offers couples massages, couples facials, manicures, lunch for two and a bottle of champagne. Private spa parties are also popular.
Photograph by Gregory Barringer, Pro Images of PA

Bottom Left: One of the mansion's Royal Grand rooms boasts a 28-foot-high beadboard turret surrounding the Jacuzzi.
Photograph by John Richnavsky, Moods Image Photography & Video

Facing Page: Frank Buhl built this 1890 castle, which is listed on the National Register of Historic Places, as a wedding present for his bride, Julia.
Photograph by Gregory Barringer, Pro Images of PA

disrepair over the years—having become apartments and home to various businesses—and eventually was abandoned. After the steel industry recession, the town of Sharon also experienced an economic downturn and did not allot the funds to restore the once magnificent home. Her future lay in question.

In 1996, Jim and Donna Winner, owners of Tara–A Country Inn—the historic Clark, Pennsylvania, home they had lovingly purchased and restored from total abandonment—acted on an urge to save this historic landmark as well. Hardworking and genuine in their own philanthropies, Jim and Donna, much like the Buhls, sought to elevate the town of Sharon with a thriving and restorative endeavor.

Buhl Mansion Guesthouse & Spa's benefactors have done more that. Jim and Donna—with the help of a dedicated staff including niece and general manager Laura Ackley—have evolved the former residence into one of America's top-rated bed-and-breakfasts. The 10 spectacular guestrooms and the full-service spa stand as testament to Donna's talented designing acumen and her dream of exceeding every guest's expectations of luxury and service. Elegant guestrooms with fireplaces and Jacuzzis and a world-class spa offer the ultimate in luxury and pampering. In addition to a bed-and-breakfast, the inn also houses Winner Art Gallery. This attention to each detail keeps guests coming back, as well as travelers from all over the country, seeking their accommodations.

Built around a history of love and renewal, Buhl Mansion offers the perfect mix of romance and serenity for guests; in fact the mansion has been ranked as one of America's top 10 most romantic inns. And whether one's idea of an escape includes a day of luxury in the spa, shopping, golf or spending the entire day in bed beginning with a fabulous breakfast, the staff at Buhl Mansion make it their priority to be at their guests' beck and call 24-hours a day. Because the entire castle and its grounds can be acquired exclusively for an impressive corporate retreat or one-of-a-kind wedding among the lush gardens, the Sharon, Pennsylvania, castle is the perfect destination to make guests feel like royalty.

Above: Mr. Buhl's Den captures the allure of the Old World luxury this steel baron once enjoyed. Guests can now indulge in the same sense of royalty.
Photograph by John Richnavsky, Moods Image Photography & Video

Facing Page Top: This Victorian greenhouse amidst seven and a half acres of formal gardens is an idyllic background and venue for many special events and castle weddings.
Photograph by Laura Ruppersberger Photography

Facing Page Bottom: Guests imbibe champagne and bask in the elegance of the spa's reception area. This world-class spa offers the ultimate in luxury and pampering.
Photograph by Gregory Barringer, Pro Images of PA

The Captain Lord Mansion

Kennebunkport, Maine

*D*uring the War of 1812, Nathaniel Lord, a wealthy shipbuilder, was on a commercial hiatus after British blockades cut off New England trade. The good captain needed something to do, and so he had his idle shipwrights construct The Captain Lord Mansion overlooking the river in Kennebunkport, Maine. Seven generations of Lords lived in the large home, until 1972, when it was converted to senior housing.

In 1978, Rick Litchfield and Bev Davis were looking for a door out of the corporate world. Initially looking for a restaurant to run, the two saw a high divorce rate in that business; so they passed. When they saw the opportunity waiting at the mansion, they jumped.

Kennebunkport at the time was quiet, not the destination hot spot that it is today. It was primarily a summertime spot—the other nine months were sleepy. But the couple sensed the fortuitousness; the Mansion had lots of rooms, had a food service license and, more importantly, had potential. "It didn't seem so risky when we were younger," says Rick. They rode the bed-and-breakfast wave, surviving a nail-biting pair of gas crises. And they continue to ride on.

Rick and Bev personally operate both of the mansion's Federal-style buildings—The Captain Lord Mansion and The Captain's Garden House. While Rick manages the administrative side, Bev focuses on decorating and managing the housekeeping—an arrangement that has worked well for the past 30 years.

The 20,000-square-foot Captain Lord Mansion offers 16 rooms of choice. The Captain's Garden House encompasses four additional rooms where guests escape their busy lives for a relaxing vacation or a romantic, celebratory weekend getaway at this attractive inn. Accommodations at The Captain Lord Mansion are meticulously decorated and designed to offer a serene interlude filled with special romantic touches.

Top Left: One of many fine European paintings adorns a room at the inn.
Photograph by Warren Jagger

Second Left: The slipper-foot jet tub is in the Americana guestroom.
Photograph by Warren Jagger

Third Left: Nathaniel and Phebe Lord, the original owners of the mansion, greet guests as they arrive at the inn.
Photograph by Warren Jagger

Bottom Left: One of the inn's attractive gas fireplaces warms a guestroom.
Photograph by Warren Jagger

Facing Page: A view looks across the River Green toward The Captain Lord Mansion.
Photograph by Warren Jagger

Guests celebrate and indulge in the timeless elegance of one of the large, beautifully appointed and exceptionally detailed mansion guestrooms. Each one pampers the senses. Relax and enjoy the many luxurious amenities. Snuggle into a richly decorated and incredibly comfortable oversized four-poster bed. Luxuriate in fine linens amid piles of pillows. Feel the warmth of a cozy gas fireplace that flickers just beyond the bed. Retreat to one of the marvelous private baths and bask in the tranquility of a double whirlpool tub; relax with an invigorating hydro-massage body jet shower; enjoy the comforts of a heated marble floor. This romantic guestroom atmosphere is complemented by fresh flowers and fine European art.

Guests may come for the rooms, but they will also be impressed with the breakfasts. The mansion offers a full breakfast, prepared by three fine cooks. Among the varieties of delectable breakfast items are the choice organic yogurts, fresh fruit and baked goods. Entrées include French toast stuffed with raspberry cream cheese, Belgian waffles with Maine blueberry preserves and fine Maine maple syrup, spinach soufflé or frittatas. Freshly squeezed Florida orange juice, flavored coffee and, on colder days, Swedish glogg provide a veritable symphony for the stomach.

These days, Kennebunkport draws a variety of people—empty nesters, long weekenders, whale watchers, lobster cruisers; there are classic sailboats to ride, spectacular bicycle trails and championship golf courses. Only a short ways off is The White Barn, a five-diamond, AAA restaurant, as well as plenty of shopping, art galleries and museums, including the world's best trolley museum. And, of course, there are the Bushes—Walker's Point is five minutes from the inn. The Captain Lord Mansion has recently added a day spa, which features massages from a therapeutic massage company with more than 25 years' experience. So whether the back or the soul is in need of respite, The Captain Lord Mansion is New England comfort at its finest.

Above: Ship Lincoln is one of the inn's original master bedrooms.
Photograph by Warren Jagger

Facing Page Top Left: Custom baths, heated marble floors and robes abound.
Photograph by Warren Jagger

Facing Page Top Right: Excellent lighting, comfortable sitting areas and four-poster beds create a sumptuous escape.
Photograph by Warren Jagger

Facing Page Bottom: Serenity, warmth and luxury surround guests in the mansion's gathering room.
Photograph by Warren Jagger

Christmas Farm Inn and Spa

Jackson, New Hampshire

Visit Christmas Farm Inn and Spa in winter, and you just might think you stepped into a Currier & Ives print. Indeed, the inn's rustic architecture and idyllic setting radiate the feeling of an earlier, simpler America. More than two centuries old, the structures themselves are steeped in a rich history, one that lives on through local records and oral tradition as well as in the inn itself. Situated in the quaint village of Jackson, New Hampshire—known as one of the top 10 romantic destinations in the country—and surrounded by White Mountain National Forest, the rural retreat lives up to its name, evocative of the magic of Christmas, the simplicity and abundance of a country farm and the restorative power of a spa enveloped in the romance of the past.

Guests of Christmas Farm Inn stay in one of the inn's five settings, each of which possesses unique qualities and a fascinating narrative. The front portion of the Main Inn was constructed in 1786 as a homestead, replacing the 1778 Saltbox, which became a storage space and, for a time, served as the village jail. The back of the Main Inn was added in the 1800s, when the Free Will Baptist Church was transported on logs via oxen from its location up the road and attached to the main structure. The Barn has been dated around the same time as the Main Inn and boasts hand-hewn beams, original mortise-and-tenon pegged joints, cathedral ceilings and a granite fireplace. Various cottages that pepper the property along the inn's winding road are available for couples and small families, and the most recent addition, the Carriage House, is a dose of the new millennium, with luxury suites, an indoor pool and a full-service, state-of-the-art spa.

The property passed through several hands before Dana and Cathi Belcher and their children took responsibility in 2007. Having been in their family for nearly 10 years, the inn held particular appeal for the Belchers, who also own and operate the Lodge at Jackson Village. Delighted by the

Top Left: Christmas Farm Inn offers magical moments with Santa at the North Pole as well as much-anticipated rides on the famous Polar Express.
Photograph by BelieveinBooks.org

Second Left: Dana and Cathi Belcher, owners and innkeepers, personally greet guests upon their arrival and enjoy visiting with them throughout their stay.
Photograph by Billy McVicker

Bottom Left: Afternoon tea and homemade cookies are served by a crackling wood fire in the 1786 Main Inn's living room.
Photograph by Brooks Dodge

Facing Page & Third Left: Cross-country skiing and snowshoeing are available right from the inn. The vast trail system of the Jackson Ski Touring Foundation is the largest and most celebrated in the Northeast.
Photograph by Tim Shellmer

opportunity to share Christmas Farm's history and charm with guests the world over, Dana and Cathi have worked to revitalize the inn, emphasizing its namesake qualities. A genuine farm girl who grew up spinning, weaving, making soap and cooking on a woodburning stove, Cathi brings her passion for farm-fresh ingredients to the table. Each meal, from the lavish country breakfast buffet to the gourmet made-from-scratch desserts, is prepared by the inn's chefs from ingredients picked daily from the organic herb and vegetable gardens, complemented by the inn's *Wine Spectator* Award of Excellence-winning wine list.

In addition to cultivating the wholesomeness of farm life, Dana and Cathi strive to capture the excitement and anticipation of Christmas year-round in every aspect of the inn. A true winter wonderland, Jackson typifies the spirit of the holidays, and a visit to this quintessential New England Village is equivalent to stepping back in time and into a Norman Rockwell painting. A blanket of snow covers the town's sloping steeples, covered bridge and abundant pines as well as the nearby White Mountains. If the setting were not enough, the town has become widely renowned for its yearly enactment of Chris Van Allsburg's *The Polar Express*. The original event based on the classic Christmas story, the North Conway, New Hampshire, Polar Express Event is a family experience described by many as the best of their lives. Children board the train in pajamas, where elves— volunteers from across the county—serve them hot cocoa and lead them in Christmas carols. When the train arrives at the North Pole, an actor playing the boy from the book, now grown, reads the story to a rapt audience.

Top Right: The inn boasts the largest outdoor pool in the county as well as one of Mount Washington Valley's few indoor pools, hot tubs and health and fitness centers.
Photograph by Brooks Dodge

Bottom Right: Plum Pudding Restaurant offers a hearty country breakfast buffet or a candlelight dinner for two, while Mistletoe Pub serves lighter fare.
Photograph by Brooks Dodge

Facing Page: An authentic New England experience at the historic post-and-beam barn makes family reunions, weddings and corporate functions truly memorable.
Photograph by Brooks Dodge

After the reading, Santa greets each child, and then they re-board the train to return to the station, where each receives a silver bell.

Begun in 1995, this annual tradition now engages hundreds of area volunteers and draws families from across the globe—many of whom take advantage of Christmas Farm Inn's Polar Express Packages. Exciting though it is, the event is merely one of many enticing activities in and around Jackson. A premier destination for skiers, Jackson is the site of the country's longest-running Alpine ski slope and has been rated the number one cross-country ski center in the eastern United States—whose beginnings were birthed in Christmas Farm Inn's own living room. The fun does not stop when ski season ends, as the area provides ample opportunities for hiking, cycling and kayaking through the scenic mountains. Families can live out classic bedtime tales at Story Land theme park, enjoy scenic sky rides and the thrill of the Wildcat Mountain ZipRider. If indoor sports are more to your liking, innkeeper Dana Belcher explains that "Jackson is only eight miles and half a century away" from North Conway's famous discount and tax-free shopping.

Couples enjoy covered sleigh rides and quiet strolls through Jackson's Nestlenook Victorian village, or pamper themselves with rejuvenating treatments at the inn's very fine Carriage House spa—a longtime village tradition as, for more than 100 years, people have traveled to its indigenous mineral springs for their healing powers. When the day's activities come to an end, Christmas Farm guests return to the inn's Mistletoe Pub, where they can enjoy pub fare and signature drinks, such as the chocolate peppermint martini complete with a candy cane swizzle stick.

With all that Christmas Farm Inn and Spa has to offer, it is little wonder that it has sustained vibrant activity for more than two centuries. With the Belcher family's genuine love for the inn and its guests, the spirit of Christmas Farm will carry on for many years forward.

Above: Sometimes referred to as "Norman Rockwellville," Jackson, New Hampsire, is everything one would expect from a historic and picturesque New England village, replete with a white-steepled church and a famous covered bridge.
Photograph by Bob Grant

Facing Page Top: The Carriage House, home to a state-of-the-art spa and luxurious living areas, pampers body and soul into complete relaxation.
Photograph by Brooks Dodge

Facing Page Bottom: With breathtaking views of nearby Mount Washington, 12 luxury suites are the ultimate in comfortable, top-of-the-line lodging for both short and extended stays.
Photograph by Brooks Dodge

Deerfield Inn

Deerfield, Massachusetts

*T*aking a leisurely stroll down Old Main Street is an experiential step back in time where visitors feel the slower pace and graciousness of colonial days gone by. The almost 350-year-old town of Deerfield, Massachusetts, is a designated National Historic Landmark, home to museums, preserved historical residences and the beloved Deerfield Inn. Nestled in the heart of one of New England's most charming villages, the inn is a retreat for romantics and urban dwellers alike who desire the chance to simply unwind. Elegant and comfortable with a richly documented heritage, Deerfield Inn opened its doors in 1884, and present-day innkeepers Jane and Karl Sabo continue to offer the utmost in hospitality. Surrounded by more than 1,000 acres of scenic vistas, open farmland and rolling hills in the Pioneer Valley of western Massachusetts, the full-service inn offers fresh air, fresh produce and a fresh perspective for travelers from near and far.

The inn's delectable cuisine includes hearty breakfasts, light lunches in the Terrace Café, afternoon tea and cookies in the Beehive Parlor and gourmet dinners paired with affordable and diverse wine selections. As seasons change, produce from regional farmers becomes central to the chef's menu—winter root vegetables may enhance a lamb shank entrée or wild mushroom Bordelaise sauce may accompany a filet mignon. Indian pudding made from a colonial Deerfield recipe is a house specialty. The tavern, where the innkeepers' dog often mingles with patrons, is a lively place; its bar boasts single-malt whiskeys, local microbrewery ales and premium wine.

Guests return regularly to enjoy the relaxing, restorative ambience of reading by the flickering fireplace, rocking on the porch, visiting with friends and family and touring the Historic Deerfield and Memorial Hall museums. Some of the guests' most memorable and cherished moments at this classic country inn are meeting local residents, conversing with friendly museum docents and getting to know family farmers who have worked the area's fertile land for generations.

Top Left: Travelers escape the bustling city and are transported to yesteryear—the inn is perfect for relaxing and unwinding.
Photograph by Greg M. Cooper

Second Left: Guests look forward to special moments such as afternoon tea, elegantly served in delicate china and sure to soothe all of the senses.
Photograph by Greg M. Cooper

Third Left: Chocolate-dipped strawberries and a toast of chilled champagne will sweetly rekindle romance or simply indulge the taste buds.
Photograph by Greg M. Cooper

Bottom Left: Gastronomical delights are deftly prepared and presented in an atmosphere of casual fine dining, tastily complemented by a diverse wine selection.
Photograph by Greg M. Cooper

Facing Page: Nestled in the heart of a 17th-century New England village, with its slower pace and graciousness of days gone by, this historic inn offers guests a truly memorable experience.
Photograph by Greg M. Cooper

Devonfield Inn

Lee, Massachusetts

*I*n a momentous move from Miami Beach to Massachusetts, Ronnie and Bruce Singer took a giant leap of faith and left their successful city careers to become owners of Devonfield Inn, one of the region's quintessential New England inns—one that has captured their hearts and ultimately transformed their lives. This spacious 32-acre estate in the Berkshire Mountains was established more than 200 years ago and is now home to its owners, visiting guests from neighboring states and many European travelers. The landmark inn is served by the Hartford and Albany airports, making it easily reachable within a one-hour drive—New York and Boston are less than a two-and-a-half-hour drive.

The stately English country inn is situated only two miles from the picturesque historic village of Stockbridge, home of the famed Norman Rockwell Museum, and less than five minutes from Main Street in downtown Lee. This exquisite Federal-style residence was renovated and expanded in the 1930s and officially became an inn in 1980. Ardent preservationists, the present-day proprietors have maintained the original character with antique wood floors, handsome built-ins and picture windows, and they have gradually enhanced the property with central air conditioning, updated baths and modern amenities to entice the most experienced traveler.

Accommodating up to 30 guests, the inn presents six well-appointed rooms with luxurious quilts and down comforters, three suites and a freestanding cottage, some with woodburning fireplaces, flat-screen televisions and bubbling whirpool baths. A guest pantry is brimming with a selection of soothing teas, homemade cookies and pastries, hot chocolate and popcorn snacks; china and crystal intended for everyday use gleams on the shelves. As an elegant touch, upon arrival, guests receive cognac and cordials, superb handmade chocolates and fine terry robes. Gourmet breakfasts are served by candlelight: crème brûlée French toast, orange yogurt pancakes or, perhaps, a fresh artichoke frittata. The inn's rich antique décor, inviting atmosphere and gracious hospitality are unforgettable—every day etches wonderful memories that guests cherish long after their stay.

Top Left: The porch overlooks the inn's 32 acres where guests enjoy tennis, archery or the peace of a secluded hammock and a snooze.
Photograph by Al Ricketts

Bottom Left: Wintertime at the pristine Devonfield Inn affords cross-country skiing, snowshoeing or relaxing by one of the establishment's woodburning fireplaces.
Photograph by Bruce Singer

Facing Page: The natural beauty of the Berkshires is best explored with a picnic basket from the inn.
Photograph by Al Ricketts

The Berkshires resort region is a cultural arts mecca, featuring great symphony, theater and dance performances; museums, galleries and historical points of interest; world-class golf and nature trails, as well as gourmet dining, antiques and boutique shopping. Tanglewood, Jacob's Pillow and the Berkshire Theater Festival are just a few of the renowned performing arts venues. A heated swimming pool and tennis court grace the picnic-perfect premises; touring bicycles and an archery target are always available. Leisure time can also be enjoyed horseback riding or hot air ballooning, and luxury spas offer stress-relieving pampering. Winter sports are plentiful, so the inn supplies snowshoes and sleds for invigorating recreation—cross-country skiers can glide on snowfields, and downhill ski slopes are just a short drive away.

Above: Surrounded by lush, tranquil gardens, the heated pool is open from Memorial Day weekend through the end of summer.
Photograph by Gregory Cherin

Left: Steeped in history, 200-year-old Devonfield Inn has been lovingly restored to preserve the past while offering the finest modern amenities.
Photograph by Gregory Cherin

Above all, a rich sense of history is felt upon entering Devonfield Inn. Considered one of the grand "Berkshire Cottages," the inn has hosted distinguished visitors including Queen Wilhelmina of the Netherlands and Franklin D. Roosevelt in 1942. Every guest of the inn is treated like royalty, and those who return—many three to four times a year—say that they feel as though they are in someone's beautiful, private home. The spacious living room showcases a baby grand piano to play, and the hospitality includes a menu book of fine restaurants with concierge service gladly provided for dining and all sorts of activities.

A true respite from everyday worries, the exclusive inn is often a romantic destination—an extraordinary place where marriage proposals, weddings, anniversaries and family reunions are celebrated year-round. It is quite fitting that Devonfield Inn has been honored as Inn of the Year 2008 in Pamela Lanier's famed international guide to specialty lodging.

Top Right: Replete with an abundance of windows, the penthouse suite's panes frame views of the estate and the tops of towering pines, creating the sense of being in a tree house.
Photograph by Al Ricketts

Bottom Right: Cream and rust-colored floral wallcoverings bring the estate's panoramas into the sun-dappled Sedgewick Suite.
Photograph by Al Ricketts

The English Inn

Eaton Rapids, Michigan

*I*magine an inn where the Old World flavor of Europe and the legendary romance of the English countryside commingle to offer a most relaxing and alluring experience. Tucked amid the woodlands overlooking the picturesque Grand River is a magnificent Tudor Revival mansion, a 1927 historic landmark that has been lovingly preserved by innkeepers Gary and Donna Nelson for the ultimate benefit of their fortunate visitors. This 15-acre estate with fragrant, formal English gardens is only eight miles from the capital city of Lansing and is known to be one of the most hospitable inns of the Midwest.

The English Inn was once a stately private residence built and owned by Oldsmobile executive, Irving Reuter. Designated as a state historic landmark building, this authentic Tudor-style residence was originally transformed into a bed-and-breakfast in 1989—acquired, restored and improved since 1996 by its current owners. A feast for the eyes and the senses, the beautiful estate includes the classical two-story stucco inn with its black marble fireplace and baby grand piano, as well as several private cottages on manicured grounds. An equally regal, French-inspired 10,000-square-foot, full-service banquet and convention facility called Medovue Hall was added to the property in 2002. Regional businesses frequently host retreats and conferences here, and the elegant ballroom can accommodate up to 250 guests for corporate banquets and lavish wedding receptions. A romantic getaway destination designed for couples young and old, the established inn is most renowned in the region for its inviting, friendly atmosphere, splendid English-country accommodations, richly appointed rooms with fireplaces and Jacuzzi baths, as well as award-winning dining. Guests are also able to enjoy an evening of theater or sounds of the symphony at performing arts venues on the nearby Michigan State University campus and BoarsHead Theatre in Lansing.

Top Left: The lions' view from the back terrace overlooks formal English gardens, a tournament-size croquet court and a well-manicured lawn extending to the Grand River.
Photograph by Doug Elbinger

Second Left: The view of Medovue Hall overlooks the gardens.
Photograph courtesy of The English Inn

Third Left: Countless weddings and receptions—ranging from 10 to 250 guests—are celebrated on the grounds or at the adjacent Medovue Hall.
Photograph by Doug Elbinger

Bottom Left: Mature-growth trees are punctuated with seasonal plantings of brightly hued flowers.
Photograph courtesy of The English Inn

Facing Page: The stately English Tudor country house greets guests as they arrive through the gated entryway.
Photograph by David Parsons

Four dining rooms and an English pub are bustling with gourmet food preparation every day of the week; a formally trained culinary staff create elaborate three-course breakfasts, light lunches and dinner cuisine with house specialties such as a delectable Chateaubriand for two and fresh Indiana duck with Michigan sundried cherry sauce. The formal Devonshire Dining Room is the largest of all, and its distinctive wine list has received the annual *Wine Spectator*'s Award of Excellence for more than a decade; the wood-paneled Dickens Pub with its casual ambience serves ale, single-malt Scotch and authentic British fare of fish-and-chips and shepherd's pie.

Possessing an understated elegance and offering impeccable service, the beautiful inn has hosted numerous wedding receptions, both large and small. Vow ceremonies are held at the pergola overlooking the river, at the rose trellis in the upper garden, in the banquet hall or framed by the inn's fireplace. The surrounding grounds feature a serene fishpond and charming gazebo, an artesian well, colorful annual and perennial gardens, a tournament-size croquet court on the lawn and many nature trails—an extraordinary place where the fabled English countryside becomes a dream come true.

Keeping with the inn's tradition of creating special memories, personal celebrations are toasted every day— unforgettable weddings, milestone birthdays, happy anniversaries, first prom dates and magical marriage proposals have all occurred within the inn's garden walls. Those who have visited return again and again, as the idyllic setting is perfect for the romantic moments and significant gatherings of life.

Top Right: Garden and river views are enjoyed from the back of the inn.
Photograph by Michael's Studio of Lansing

Bottom Right: The terrace overlooks the gardens as well as the Grand River.
Photograph by Michael's Studio of Lansing

Facing Page Top: The transition from the foyer into the main Devonshire Dining Room reveals Honduran mahogany-paneled walls and an Italian-marble fireplace.
Photograph courtesy of The English Inn

Facing Page Bottom Left: Mrs. Reuters' favorite color—lavender—is featured in the Somerset's guestroom.
Photograph by David Parsons

Facing Page Bottom Right: Named after the royal family, the Windsor Room has a striking rose granite fireplace.
Photograph by David Parsons

Fairthorne Cottage
Bed & Breakfast

Cape May, New Jersey

An enchanting, seaside Victorian village, Cape May, New Jersey, is an idyllic, one-of-a-kind vacation destination along the Atlantic Coast. Former presidents Franklin Pierce, Chester A. Arthur and Ulysses S. Grant were well-known for passing leisurely summer days in this engaging environment—the oldest seaside resort in the United States—more than a century-and-a-half ago. Many folks have come and gone since those bygone, 19th-century summer days, but little has changed in this charming locale, which was officially designated a National Landmark Historic city in 1976.

The consummate sojourn in Cape May includes a requisite stay at the luxurious yet unassuming Fairthorne Cottage Bed & Breakfast. Originally built in 1892 by a whaling captain, this historic inn is set right in the heart of Cape May, providing a picturesque, year-round seaside resort just moments away from the beach and ample shopping and dining opportunities. Since February of 1992, Fairthorne has been run by innkeepers Diane and Ed Hutchinson, who bought the adjacent building in 1997 and have made considerable upgrades to Fairthorne, ensuring that the Victorian ambience is augmented by the presence of modern conveniences and amenities.

Set between the Atlantic Ocean and the Delaware Bay, Cape May's setting is simply stunning, and the town's historic Victorian architecture has been impeccably preserved by the Cape May City Historic Preservation Commission. Seasonal recreation abounds, thanks to the Mid-Atlantic Center for the Arts, a local non-profit organization, which is earnestly committed to ensuring a lengthy and enticing lineup of attractions during peak tourist months. Nearly every single Cape May weekend includes the presence of unique festivals and local attractions, from celebrations of jazz, crafts and antiques to events lauding food, wine and even Sherlock Holmes. Year-round local draws include historic trolley tours through town, a restored, historic lighthouse and the 1879 Emlen Physick Estate Museum, to name a few. Of course, the beach lies just a block-and-a-half away from Fairthorne, affording convenient dolphin watching and sunbathing opportunities.

Top Left: The reflection from the Ashley Room bathroom hints at the accommodation's luxury. Light and airy, the room offers a king-sized bed, gas fireplace and a television, DVD player and CD player.
Photograph by Jumping Rocks Photography

Bottom Left: With many sumptuous breakfasts from which to choose, guests can customize their morning meals.
Photograph by Jumping Rocks Photography

Facing Page: A wraparound veranda adds to the charm of Fairthorne Cottage.
Photograph by Aleksey Moryakov

Whether the day is spent amidst charming local attractions or leisurely relaxing in Fairthorne's utopian splendor, 10 elegant and distinctive rooms ensure serene slumber at day's end. Tastefully decorated with antique furniture and Victorian-era trappings, luxury linens and impossibly soft mattresses afford the comforts of modernity. Guests awaken to delectable daily breakfast offerings deftly prepared by Diane. Alternating between a sweet breakfast that might include Belgian waffles with strawberries, fresh whipped cream and homemade muffins one day and savory breakfasts consisting of items like eggs Benedict, fresh fruit and buttermilk coffee cake the next, patrons always start the day off blissfully satiated. A wraparound veranda affords resplendent alfresco summertime dining with streetscape views, and Cape May rockers, which are renowned for their stress-relieving abilities, adorn the front porch. Diane's afternoon refreshments—iced tea, lemonade and cookies in the summer and hot tea, flavored coffee and cookies in the winter—are staples of any Fairthorne stay. The savory aromas from Diane's famous, daily-made cookies waft through the inn every afternoon, procuring sweet, mouthwatering fragrances that lure guests down to indulge in the warm, sweet divinity.

Cape May, New Jersey, is an unforgettable city redolent of a past era. Centrally located amidst breathtaking surroundings and engaging attractions is the must-visit Fairthorne Cottage Bed & Breakfast, where Diane and Ed offer impeccable hospitality, ensuring your every desire is fulfilled while providing a tranquil ambience that simply begs for another night's stay.

Above: A king-sized bed, gas fireplace and bathroom with a two-person whirlpool and tiled shower give the Gabrielle Room a great deal of comfort. A television, DVD player and CD player make the room's entertainment options endless.
Photograph by Jumping Rocks Photography

Facing Page Top: On the veranda, visitors relieve stress by spending spare time in the Cape May rockers.
Photograph by Jumping Rocks Photography

Facing Page Bottom Left: Two-room suite Emma-Kate offers a king-sized bed, a fireplace within the sitting room and a large bathroom with a two-person marble shower.
Photograph by Jumping Rocks Photography

Facing Page Bottom Right: Afternoon tea drinkers can enjoy a cup of Earl Grey while peeking into the parlor.
Photograph by Jumping Rocks Photography

The Four Columns Inn

Newfane, Vermont

*V*enturing into the picturesque early 18th-century village of Newfane, Vermont, one feels as though time has enchantingly reversed. Surrounding tourists and residents in architectural and American history, Newfane's charming town square has stood since 1825—when the threat of Native American attacks lessoned and the locals voted to relocate their town square to lower ground—and its integrity has remained nearly unaffected by the passing of the centuries. Originally founded in 1753 as Fane, Newfane bears the proud distinction of having all of its downtown buildings appear on the National Register of Historic Places. Though modern advancement has certainly not passed Newfane by, it has not managed to undermine the charm of this increasingly rare, unspoiled American gem.

While owner Bruce Pfander had been a Los Angeles entertainment industry executive and wife Debbie had been in the hospitality business for many years, they were ready for the next adventure; something they could undertake together and include the family. In 2004, they moved the family across the country and began life in New England. From that time, the Pfanders tirelessly worked to renovate, redecorate and invigorate the splendor of the inn.

The celebrated and stunning Greek Revival manor, nestled at the foot of its own private 150-acre mountain, is exactly what one would conjure when imagining the perfect New England inn. Originally built in 1832 as a homestead and established as an inn and restaurant in 1969, the property and home are decorated by lush gardens cultivated over decades of care with a meandering stream running through the grounds. Though The Four Columns Inn offers a postcard setting in a location that feels worlds away from the hustle of any city, it is easily accessible from New York, Boston and Hartford.

Top Left: The Four Columns Inn is renowned for exceptional dining. Guests are treated to a taste of culinary history at dinner and a hearty Vermont breakfast every morning.
Photograph by Rare Brick

Bottom Left: The sights are like driving into a postcard. The front porch view on the village green is much the same as when Pardon Kimball built this house in 1832.
Photograph by Jumping Rocks Photography

Facing Page: The Greek Revival architecture reflects the quiet dignity of this exceptional Village Green. The front building of the inn sparkles in the New England snow.
Photograph by Bruce Pfander

Fifteen guestrooms are elegantly decorated, yet warm and welcoming. Each room is slightly different, seamlessly integrating the allure of traditional décor with the convenience of modern amenities. The diversity in rooms also ensures that each guest has a personal experience, from lovely rooms with standard baths to deluxe and luxury suites with grand bathrooms. Each guestroom is filled with charming antiques and queen- or king-sized beds. Guestroom amenities may also include a Jacuzzi or soaking tubs, gas fireplaces, CD players, fluffy robes and luxury bath products, and for those who wish to stay connected, wireless internet is available throughout.

Renowned as one of the finest restaurants in New England from its beginning, Four Columns was founded by French Chef Rene Chardain in 1969. It is an inn to behold and has a magnificent bill of fare to complement the experience. A hearty New England breakfast is served to start guests' days off while dinner awaits at night. With a tenure at The Four Columns that began more than 30 years ago with Chef Chardain, Chef Greg Parks continues the tradition of fine dining that draws seasoned diners from around the globe. Menus change seasonally and feature classic New England selections with French and Asian influences.

For those wishing for an active respite, Newfane appeals to outdoorsmen of all bents. Winters offer fabulous skiing at Stratton and nearby resorts as well as cross-country skiing and ice skating. During the warmer months, guests enjoy hiking, kayaking, biking or a dip in the inn's pool. For those who prefer to rest and recharge, Newfane also offers nearly exertion-free activities, including wonderful antiquing, shopping and fine dining—all within a short drive. And as everyone has heard, Vermont's legendary fall foliage is among the best in the world.

Counting among its fans a list of celebrities and well-known political figures, The Four Columns Inn is a beloved destination that simply reminds its guests of all that is great about America's past and its present.

Above: Carefully maintained gardens and lawns lead to the tranquility of a rushing stream and private mountain, enjoyed by many as a place to unwind in peaceful solitude.
Photograph by Bruce Pfander

Facing Page Top: Renovations and room décor have been carefully orchestrated to surround guests with tasteful simplicity without compromising comfort, amenities or conveniences.
Photograph by Jumping Rocks Photography

Facing Page Bottom Left: Welcoming, warm and relaxing are words often used to describe the common characteristics of these uniquely diverse rooms and suites.
Photograph by Rare Brick

Facing Page Bottom Right: Craftsmanship is evident throughout the inn as Old World beauty is combined with custom woodworking and architecture to preserve and celebrate the beauty of a former era.
Photograph by Jumping Rocks Photography

Glenlaurel — A Scottish Country Inn

Hocking Hills, Ohio

"*I*t's a beautiful day at Glenlaurel!" The receptionist's voice expresses the inviting warmth and storybook allure hidden in one of the most romantic inns of the Midwest. An authentically inspired Scottish estate nestled amidst 140 acres of precious woodlands in the Hocking Hills region of southeastern Ohio less than a one-hour drive from Columbus, lovely Glenlaurel captivates all who enter. Greg and Kelley Leonard are proud innkeepers and live in the idyllic hamlet to personally ensure a memorable experience.

The Edinburgh Dining Room is the perfect setting for candlelit gourmet dinners, and the cozy Loch Ness Pub provides a club atmosphere for conviviality. In-room continental breakfast service is always available, and three remarkable chefs prepare a complete breakfast menu, mouthwatering lunches and formal five-course evening meals with rotating daily entrées.

This secluded stone and stucco inn is perched high on a ridge overlooking the privately owned Camusfearna Gorge, which is surrounded by walking trails, rock cliffs and waterfalls, making it a year-round escape that offers guests unparalleled beauty during all four seasons—guests can enjoy a stroll on the forested grounds, and nature-lovers appreciate the scenery with gentle deer and wildlife. The property also offers guests the Joppa Spa and Wellness Center, with full services including massages, body wraps and scrubs as well as guided meditations, yoga, aromatherapy, color/sound therapy and Reiki healing sessions. Whether a honeymoon, anniversary weekend, birthday, intimate wedding destination or girlfriends' getaway, Glenlaurel is laced with romance—a poetic and peaceful place to relax, rejuvenate, read or simply reflect while experiencing the true spirit of the Scottish Highlands.

Top Left: All seasons are beautiful at Glenlaurel, but autumn invites myriad leisure activities.
Photograph courtesy of Glenlaurel Inn

Second Left: The sound of Scottish music fills the air as guests are transported to another place and time where worries release upon arrival.
Photograph courtesy of Glenlaurel Inn

Third Left: The Mackenzie royal suite—as with all guest accommodations—is themed after a prominent personality from Scottish history and features a variety of comforting special amenities, including Glenlaurel's homemade shortbread cookies and fluffy, plush bathrobes.
Photograph courtesy of Glenlaurel Inn

Bottom Left: Every night at Glenlaurel is an experience to remember—the inn's gourmet cuisine with a Scottish flair is legendary. Presented exclusively on Saturday nights is a seven-course dinner with the signature roasted rack of lamb; a kilt-clad bagpiper beckons guests promptly at seven o'clock—attire is classy casual.
Photograph courtesy of Glenlaurel Inn

Facing Page: With 19 accommodations in all, the Manor House features luxurious suites and richly appointed rooms; the nearby Carriage House has one romantic suite and a cozy garret. The pinnacle experience for couples and friends is a tranquil stay in one of the 13 cottages and charming crofts.
Photograph by Ken Schory

Hydrangea House Inn

Newport, Rhode Island

When visitors are searching for a luxurious place to rest each night in Newport, Rhode Island, no place offers a more refined and sophisticated retreat than Hydrangea House Inn. With nine exquisite bedrooms that are all custom-designed, guests find themselves pampered with superior comforts. Grant Edmondson and Dennis Blair opened the inn in 1988 and say their business is more than a job—it is a passion. This intense dedication can be seen by their interaction with the inn's daily operations and distinctive style.

Each room's décor is designed around a specific fabric used in the room with luscious colors that were chosen to complement its distinct ambience. The color palette in the main areas of the inn is stunning. A lavish use of vivid cranberry, striking plum and fresh honey tones immediately tells guests they have chosen an exceptional inn.

Choosing the right name for the inn was no simple task. After searching for four months, Grant was driving along the north end of the island when he came upon a spectacular row of hydrangeas. The name Hydrangea House Inn was an instant hit. Inspired by its name, there are now 12 varieties of hydrangeas coloring the inn's gardens with their delicate red, pink, white and blue petals.

Located in the middle of Newport on historic Bellevue Avenue, the inn is surrounded by the Colonial and Gilded Age history and culture that put this town on the map. Whether guests are touring endless rows of spectacular mansions or taking long walks to enjoy the fragrance of the beach, there are endless activities sure to both enlighten and refresh.

Top Left: A bountiful, multiple-course buffet breakfast is served each morning in the exquisitely decorated dining room.
Photograph by Jumping Rocks Photography

Bottom Left: Just outside of the penthouse king suite, a private veranda awaits.
Photograph by Jumping Rocks Photography

Facing Page: Part of a row house built long ago, the inn is located in the center of historic Newport.
Photograph by Rare Brick

Guests start their day off with a bountiful, three-course breakfast that is sure to give them the energy needed for a busy day around town. While the inn's crisp fruits and hot pastries always satisfy, returning guests come back searching for a delicious plate of raspberry-stuffed fritter pancakes.

After an indulgent and one-of-a-kind breakfast, guests can get a bright look into the United States' history by taking a few walking tours through Newport, seeing and feeling the places that the earliest settlers called home. Along with exploring the pastimes of Newport, there is also the fantastic harbor to meet. The beach is a 15-minute walk from the inn; guests can spend the afternoon sailing, boating or touring the harbor.

Guests may take a deep breath after touring the town by enjoying an afternoon sampling of wine and cheese at Hydrangea House Inn. Many also take advantage of an in-suite massage or bath in one of the in-room, two-person spas, while others may simply choose to wrap themselves in a blanket next to a cozy fireplace to reflect on the day.

Whatever their method of relaxation, guests will surely be whisked into a luxurious retreat that enriches the mind and refreshes the body at Hydrangea House Inn.

Top Right: Guests gather in the drawing room to enjoy tea or a glass of wine after a day of touring Newport, the city by the sea.
Photograph by Jumping Rocks Photography

Bottom Right: The suite's bold colors are a perfect complement to its exquisite French Regency queen-sized bed.
Photograph by Jumping Rocks Photography

Facing Page Top: Hand-sewn draperies create a sumptuous, elegant feeling in this two-room suite.
Photograph by Jumping Rocks Photography

Facing Page Bottom: Amenities such as the Winter Garden Suite's welcoming spa tub are present throughout the inn.
Photograph by Jumping Rocks Photography

The Inn at Cooperstown

Cooperstown, New York

A visit to Cooperstown, New York, is a trek back to the days of yore—a return to a charming, Old World lifestyle with something for everyone, encapsulated in a quaint village nestled between a pair of valleys and moments away from shimmering Lake Otsego. Within this enchanting, historically rich hamlet, The Inn at Cooperstown, which is centrally located amid ample local attractions, is a must-stay destination for any discerning traveler fortunate enough to sojourn in this eclectic town.

Originally built in 1874 as a hotel, The Inn at Cooperstown was extensively restored in 1985 and has received continuous improvements in ensuing years. Purchased in 2003 by Marc and Sherrie Kingsley, the inn has since undergone additional enhancements and is currently in an exquisite state. Set on a half-acre lot, the inn's front yard is a significant green space, adorned with majestic chestnut and maple trees—many of which are more than 100 years old—with a garden on the north end. In fact, sitting in a rocking chair on the inn's sweeping front veranda, simply enjoying the park-like setting across the street as well as the hustle and bustle of Main Street to the south, has become a leisurely pastime at The Inn at Cooperstown.

While the National Baseball Hall of Fame and Museum is certainly the most-visited attraction in Cooperstown, there are myriad other enticing destinations nearby. The Fenimore Art Museum is home to a premier collection of American Indian art, American paintings and folk art, and The Farmers' Museum accurately depicts life from more than 150 years ago. World-class opera can be enjoyed at the renowned Glimmerglass Opera, just eight miles north of Cooperstown. For those harboring a strong affinity for choice ales, the town is home to a pair of local breweries: Brewery Ommegang and the Cooperstown Brewing Company, the former of which holds a beer-tasting event every summer known as "Belgium comes to Cooperstown." Of course, Cooperstown's natural setting is dynamic in its own right, drawing numerous out-of-towners, especially bicycling enthusiasts, for its resplendent fall foliage and buoyant springs.

Top Left: No one can resist scrumptious, homemade breakfast choices.
Photograph by Jumping Rocks Photography

Second Left: Sometimes, a quiet spot to relax and read is the best part of a weekend getaway.
Photograph by Jumping Rocks Photography

Third Left: The game table in the front parlor occupies guests for hours, conveniently situated near the cozy sitting area.
Photograph by Jumping Rocks Photography

Bottom Left: The premium suite includes a wet bar and separate seating with a flat-panel television.
Photograph by Jumping Rocks Photography

Facing Page: Open year-round, the storybook beauty of The Inn at Cooperstown is best captured in the winter.
Photograph by Jumping Rocks Photography

The village of Cooperstown affords ample outdoor activities within close proximity to the hotel as well. Situated on the south end of Otsego Lake, the inn provides convenient opportunities for nearby water recreation such as water skiing, kayaking and boat rides, just to name a few. For the avid golfer, nearby Leatherstocking Golf Course provides what many consider to be one of the most scenic and challenging resort golf courses on the East Coast. Of course, outdoor leisure is not confined only to warmer months; ice fishing, cross-country skiing, snowshoeing and area snowmobiling are all popular winter diversions. Whether the day is spent sitting leisurely on the

Above: The premium guestroom on the third floor of the inn is highlighted with rich red hues and carefully crafted décor.
Photograph by Jumping Rocks Photography

Left: Wet bars are complete with wine set-ups in the suite—a perfect way to slow down and reflect on the day's events.
Photograph by Jumping Rocks Photography

hotel's tranquil front porch, amidst the town seeing the sights or enjoying Cooperstown's exceptional outdoor recreation, guests retire to one of the inn's 17 elegant, tastefully decorated rooms at the end of the day and awake to breakfast featuring a hot entrée, muffins and locally baked bread.

An enchanting, restored historical hotel in a one-of-a-kind, four-season village, The Inn at Cooperstown is a requisite component of any noteworthy visit to this historic town.

Above: The parlors at the inn allow visitors to curl up by the fire and enjoy a movie, a sporting event or a good book.
Photograph by Jumping Rocks Photography

Right: Breakfast can be savored by the fireplace in one of the inn's two dining rooms.
Photograph by Jumping Rocks Photography

The Inn at Richmond

Richmond, Massachusetts

When the summer sun is shining, enjoy the warmth on your face as you relax in a hammock listening to the sounds of nature. As the hush of the first snowfall rests on even the tiniest branches, grab a mug of hot cocoa after spending the afternoon ice skating, snowshoeing or cross-country skiing. And when the first gusts of autumn's crisp winds fly around Richmond, Massachusetts, be awed by breathtaking colors as you explore the inn's expansive grounds. As spring begins to share its most treasured works of art, come to The Inn at Richmond to take in the delights of nature that have been quietly slumbering.

Built in 1776 on 27 acres, this gentleman's farm has a welcoming atmosphere where a remarkable alley of sugar maple trees reflecting each season beckons guests to shed their hurried lives and enjoy the peace of the country. The main house, with five guestrooms, some with fireplaces, offers a romantic setting for couples to recharge and reconnect. Four outlying cottages make for a cozy retreat or provide extra room for a family to play together.

The Inn at Richmond is a refuge where guests can relax and enjoy a quieter way of life. Patios and seating areas are tucked into nooks and crannies on the property, giving perfect secluded locations for meditation, leisurely reading or quiet conversations. Situated near the main estate is a lawn reserved for outdoor games in the summer and ice skating in the winter. A rustic game room is steps from guest quarters and is well-equipped with a pool table, card table and television for movies or video games. Beyond the traditional in-room massage, the inn offers a wide array of spa services provided by professional therapists in a space dedicated to quiet and relaxation.

Top Left: Friendly conversation and a little lemonade on the wraparound porch are perfect for a summer's day.
Photograph by Fine Line Photography

Second Left: Visitors cannot resist curling up by the fire on cold New England days.
Photograph by George Gardner

Third Left: After a full day of Berkshire activities, guests gladly snuggle in for a restful night.
Photograph by George Gardner

Bottom Left: Spending time in the lovely gardens is an ideal afternoon.
Photograph by Fine Line Photography

Facing Page: The inn is full of quiet places to enjoy a favorite book.
Photograph by George Gardner

A scrumptious breakfast of fresh fruits and warm baked goods is served each morning. Throughout the day, guests can avail themselves of complimentary refreshments in the richly appointed garden room. Sit, relax and enjoy a glass of wine or soda while taking in another spectacular view of the rolling hills just outside.

Follow the path of maple trees to the Berkshire Equestrian Center. Guests may take lessons and ride one of the inn's many horses, discovering this vast property with the sound of the horse's hooves keeping the beat. In inclement weather, enjoy riding in the newly constructed state-of-the-art indoor arena. And if traveling with your horse is appealing, beautiful overnight stalls are available.

With so much to enjoy at The Inn at Richmond, the inn itself is just the beginning. The Berkshires are renowned for world-class theater, music and museums, providing an array of cultural and entertainment options day and night. Also abundant are opportunities for hiking, kayaking, skiing and other pursuits for those who enjoy outdoor activities.

Whether guests have come to escape the relentless pace of life, to reconnect with loved ones or to find a deeper sense of wholeness and to rejuvenate, the perfect getaway is on this gentleman's farm. Listen closely—the breeze through the trees is inviting you to enjoy a visit to The Inn at Richmond.

Top Right: When autumn's colors explode, no one is immune to nature's beauty.
Photograph by Robert C. Farquharson

Bottom Right: Always a favorite gathering place, the inn is full of warm, welcoming nooks.
Photograph by George Gardner

Facing Page Top: When there is a chill in the air, guests take pleasure in the warm and sunny garden room.
Photograph by George Gardner

Facing Page Bottom: Regardless of the guests' pleasure, they have 27 acres to explore on skis, snowshoes or by horse-drawn sleigh.
Photograph by Colleen Quinn

Isaiah Jones Homestead

Sandwich, Massachusetts

With one step into Isaiah Jones Homestead, guests travel back to a place where there is time for stopping to smell the roses. And inside the main house, that is just what visitors can do. Fresh roses bought from the local market fill the house, where comfort and elegance go hand-in-hand. Built in 1849, the homestead is surrounded by towering cherry, walnut and pear trees that mirror its rich history. It was converted into a bed-and-breakfast in 1987, and in March 2007, Don and Katherine Sanderson continued its operation.

A three-course gourmet breakfast is served in an intimate dining room and guests just cannot get enough of it—from cranberry scones to crab cakes, these homemade treats are beyond irresistible. After breakfast, guests may linger in the garden among the lilies, hostas and soothing waterfall, or they can hop onto a bike trail along the Cape Cod Canal. Whatever fills guests' days, chocolate, spa robes and fireplaces will be waiting happily to greet them.

The inn's convenient location on Main Street in Sandwich, Massachusetts, allows visitors to drive in for a relaxing weekend and have no more need for a car. Museums such as the Sandwich Glass Museum and the Heritage Museums & Gardens along with numerous restaurants and shops are conveniently located within walking distance. Among its more distinctive historical facts is that Sandwich is the home of Thornton Burgess, the author of *The Adventures of Peter Cottontail*. It was in the company of this town's briar patches that Burgess wrote about the travels of that daring white-tailed rabbit.

After a few days guests find that they, too, cannot resist the unmatched pampering in a town whose antiquity surprises them around every corner.

Top Left: The garden is simple, elegant and peaceful.
Photograph by Katherine Sanderson

Second Left: The gathering room is the perfect spot to share a port or sherry with other guests in the evening.
Photograph by Jay Elliot

Bottom Left: The Victorian Rooms and Suites are furnished with lovely antiques and fine reproductions.
Photograph by Jay Elliot

Facing Page: The Carriage House Suites overlook the garden and fish pond.
Photograph by Katherine Sanderson

The Lafayette Inn

Easton, Pennsylvania

Historical charm meets modern-day luxury at Laura and Paolo Di Liello's bed-and-breakfast, The Lafayette Inn, which is situated on a beautiful piece of property in a quiet, Easton, Pennsylvania, neighborhood. Due to its renown as well as its prime location within walking distance from one college and a short distance from five others, the inn attracts guests from all walks of life: current and prospective college students and their families, visiting professors, guest speakers, touring musicians, business professionals, newcomers in the process of house hunting and vacationers from across the United States as well as overseas. Some stay for a night, others make it their home away from home for weeks at a time, and many return on a regular basis. The Di Liellos searched far and wide for a place special enough to entice them to take a permanent sabbatical from their high-power careers as electrical engineers, and just as they fell in love with The Lafayette Inn, so too do the scores of guests who have had the opportunity to acquaint themselves with the property and the area's myriad attractions.

Built as a mansion in 1895, the delightful Georgian-style structure has been decorated, remodeled, repurposed, cared for and touched by the hands of many. Around the time of the Great Depression, it was divided into apartments and later on it functioned as a fraternity house, but by the late 1980s it had fallen into disrepair. A group of architects and builders rallied together to save the historic mansion from being torn down, and it was extensively renovated and established as The Lafayette Inn a short time later.

The Di Liellos live next door to their 18-room bed-and-breakfast and personally ensure that each guest's stay, whether intended for relaxation or reconnecting, is more than what he or she had in mind. All of the rooms boast custom décor and an ambience that feels like home, only better. Many of the rooms have a balcony, fireplace, sitting room, oversized soaking or whirlpool

Top Left: A third-floor traditional room features a cozy windowseat and skylight.
Photograph by Jumping Rocks Photography

Second Left: The tranquil wraparound porch and delightful sunroom offer seating options for the delicious, full breakfasts.
Photograph by Jumping Rocks Photography

Third Left: This two-room suite features a daybed overlooking the private balcony—the perfect spot for enjoying morning coffee or an afternoon glass of wine.
Photograph by Jumping Rocks Photography

Bottom Left: The fire offers a place to warm up, preferably with tea and homemade cookies.
Photograph by Jumping Rocks Photography

Facing Page: The sun-dappled slate patio with a tranquil water feature is perfect for relaxing with refreshments or reading a book.
Photograph by Jumping Rocks Photography

tub; the traditional rooms are equally inviting and in-room massage is available for all, as are flowers, chocolates, snacks and romance packages. While the husband-wife innkeepers have already added personal touches to the inn in the few years since they acquired the property, they look forward to further weaving in mementos from their travels and residencies abroad—the couple has lived in Japan and Italy; Paolo was born in Naples, Italy; and both are fluent in the romantic language of Italian. Evidenced by the warm reception that each guest receives, the inn is their life, their hobby, their passion, and it makes the best of their shared architecture and design interests as well as their individual talents—Paolo's handyman skills and Laura's wizardry in the kitchen.

Above Left: The premier bathroom features pampering amenities, with an oversized soaking tub, separate shower and cozy spa robes.
Photograph by Jumping Rocks Photography

Above Right: Unique décor gives each room its own personality. Many feature stunning antique headboards and armoires.
Photograph by Jumping Rocks Photography

Left: A breakfast delivered to the room presents a perfect opportunity to cozy up next to the suite fireplace.
Photograph by Jumping Rocks Photography

The inn overflows with delightful spaces, from the gracious porch that greets guests to the parlor—where the fireplace glows with warmth, countless card games have been played and fine cheese and beverages are served in the early evening—to the sunroom that, rain or shine, is a great place to be with its three sides of glass and has elicited countless comments to the effect of "I want to take this sunroom home and attach it to the back of my house." The place where pleasant conversations are had, the sunroom doubles as a breakfast room—nothing says good morning like a made-to-order omelet from the kitchen of chef Laura or a daily changing offering of delicious homemade cakes and muffins.

Serving as the concierges, the Di Liellos are happy to point guests to numerous regional attractions, starting with restaurants; from casual taverns, grill houses and pizzerias to fine Italian, sushi, steak and seafood venues, there is no shortage of tasty cuisine. Those drawn to all things historical are in for a treat as Easton dates back to the time of the Revolutionary War. A claim to the town's fame, the Declaration of Independence was read on July 8, 1776 in its Central Square, and its version of the stars and stripes, which is on display at the public library, is believed to pre-date the one stitched by Betsy Ross. A few minutes south, the Bucks County 12-stop tour of century-old covered bridges is a unique point of interest. Outdoor activities include hiking, biking, fly-fishing, gliding through water in a mule-drawn canal boat, hot air ballooning, exploring stalagmites and stalactites at the Lost River Caverns, discovering underwater life at Dutch Springs, racing down the tracks of one of the East Coast's fastest rollercoasters at Dorney Park & Wildwater Kingdom and skiing the Poconos. The Crayola Factory and steam train rides are fun for the whole family, while plenty of upscale venues await patrons of the arts: museums, art galleries, antique shops, theaters and music festivals.

Whatever the destination of the day or sightseeing schedule of the week, all are anxious to return to the hospitable ambience of The Lafayette Inn—a destination unto itself. Guests often equate their stay at the historical haven enveloped by tall trees to visiting a dear family member who has a really large house.

Above: The parlor plays host to quiet reading time by the fire, afternoon snacks, board games and reconnecting with loved ones.
Photograph by Jumping Rocks Photography

The Lodge
at Moosehead Lake

Greenville, Maine

One of the world's most captivating hideaways in inland Maine overlooks the breathtakingly beautiful, pristine waters of Moosehead Lake. The Lodge at Moosehead Lake is an ultra-private, four-season luxury inn considered to be the epitome of "rustic sophistication"—once one has experienced the first-class accommodations, pampering hospitality and attention to detail within its doors, this description is easily grasped.

Many guests drive up from neighboring New England cities, but the charming inn can also be reached by private plane or a commercial flight into Bangor with a scenic one-and-a-half-hour drive. Nestled in the wilderness of Maine's North Woods perched high atop Blair Hill is this stately 1917 Cape Cod residence-turned-country inn. Its historical appeal has been preserved and treasured, from cozy natural stone fireplaces to the vibrant red-stained shutters that accent the front façade. The moment guests arrive, they see the warm and welcoming timeless inn, feel the fresh air fill their lungs and have a joyful tranquility wash over them as they are taken on a tour by innkeepers Linda and Dennis Bortis. Inspired by memories of many vacations in Maine, these adventuresome entrepreneurs acquired the established inn in 2007, and their passion clearly shows.

This award-winning, AAA four-diamond bed-and-breakfast destination beckons guests with well-appointed rooms and exquisite suites, gourmet cuisine in the Lakeview Dining Room and libations in the friendly pub. Breakfast fare includes German apple pancakes topped with a sweet cider reduction and raspberries—a recipe that Dennis has perfected. The inn's renowned chef, Jack Neal, prepares an elegant dinner menu of gastronomical delights paired with complementary selections from the wine cellar. And, of course, a special guest pantry is well-stocked with an array of favorite snacks as well as popular movies. Unexpected signature treats accompany guests: A thermos of steaming hot cocoa is graciously supplied on a snow-filled day trip, and Moose-A-Lix trail mix provides healthy energy for hikers.

Top Left: Moose sightings are the highlight of many trips to the lodge. The best times to see moose are mid-May through October via a guided moose safari.
Photograph by Big Deahl Productions

Bottom Left: Autumn overlooking Moosehead Lake is one of many spectacular views from the lodge. Every season is different and more beautiful than the last.
Photograph by The Lodge at Moosehead Lake

Facing Page: Guests enjoy warm summer days surrounded by gardens designed to bloom all season long.
Photograph by The Lodge at Moosehead Lake

Distinguished in Karen Brown's guide as Most Romantic Inn 2007, The Lodge at Moosehead Lake is a place where relaxation and romance go hand-in-hand. Honeymooners and partners are enchanted by the inn's casual elegance and its natural setting amidst more than seven acres of open meadow, brilliant wildflowers and gardens in the summer, treed mountain views with reds and bronzes in autumn and snowy blue-gray vistas in winter. Stresses melt away, and people return to their mellow centers from the views alone, enjoyed from the richly furnished guestrooms and suites. A masseuse is available for the ultimate unwinding, but a full range of leisure activities engages lovers of the outdoors. Alpine and cross-country skiing, snowshoeing and snowmobiling make it a winter wonderland; hiking, canoeing, kayaking, white-water rafting, fly-fishing and moose safaris led by registered guides are main attractions during summer months and into the fall.

Whether visiting for a romantic getaway, invigorating recreation or a reflective walk in the woods, a return to nature is guaranteed, all with an atmosphere of luxury and the comforts of a quintessential New England hotel. Guests have so many experiences to relish, from an inviting bed and refreshing spa bath to scrumptious meals and the pièce de résistance—a soft-as-silk cuddle from Chloé, the innkeepers' endearing French bulldog.

Top Right: The moose room in the main lodge features one-of-a-kind hand-carved beds with a sitting area and fireplace. The room has a second-floor sweeping view of Moosehead Lake and Moose Mountain.
Photograph by The Lodge at Moosehead Lake

Bottom Right: The majesty of the loon is celebrated on this hand-carved four-poster queen bed with rich bedding and blissful surroundings.
Photograph by The Lodge at Moosehead Lake

Facing Page Top: Fine dining is always the standard—here, the Lakeview Dining Room is handsomely appointed for a New Year's Eve meal.
Photograph by The Lodge at Moosehead Lake

Facing Page Bottom Left: The great room in the main lodge provides a warm and relaxing atmosphere for conversing, reading or enjoying a drink prior to dinner.
Photograph by The Lodge at Moosehead Lake

Facing Page Bottom Right: Guests' hearts are warmed as they snuggle up next to the woodburning fireplace.
Photograph by The Lodge at Moosehead Lake

The Sayre Mansion

Bethlehem, Pennsylvania

In 1858, an impressive Gothic Revival-style mansion was built by one of the community's most distinguished men and chief engineer of the Lehigh Valley Railroad, Robert Heysham Sayre. Eventually the mansion evolved into a bed-and-breakfast, which the Genzlinger family frequented while visiting their son at nearby Lehigh University. Bethlehem has always drawn business and tourists, whether visitors of the university, the famed outdoor musical festival or those in town to enjoy the holidays in the city deemed Christmastown, USA, since 1937. In an idyllic setting rich in American history, the family jumped at the chance to acquire the inn when the property became available in 2002. Already owners of a celebrated Hawley, Pennsylvania, bed-and-breakfast, they turned the business into a family affair when daughter and co-owner Carrie Ohlandt took charge of The Sayre Mansion.

Today, The Sayre Mansion offers all the amenities of a modern hotel with a blend of Old World elegance and full corporate services. Each of the 18 beautifully restored Victorian rooms is unique in design and appearance, but all come with a full, hearty breakfast, complimentary hors d'oeuvres and the gracious attention of the staff—in fact, the innkeepers for both the main house and Carriage House live on the property.

The refurbished family-friendly Carriage House has a varied history and features architectural elements as unique as the main house. The interior spaces retain the original walls and 1858 floors, and reuse almost all of the original lumber for stairs, trim and living areas, retaining the historical ambience and "living quarters" feel of the original building. The bath areas were carefully designed to use many of the original architectural elements and to provide two-person whirlpools and showers for comfort. All main house and Carriage House suites also feature feather beds, feather pillows and comforters as well as deluxe triple sheeting for the ultimate in luxury. In the 150 years since the mansion's construction, much has certainly changed, but the importance of comfort and hospitality at The Sayre Mansion will always remain.

Top Left: Breakfast, served each morning in the charming dining room, includes traditional selections and farm-fresh eggs.
Photograph by Rare Brick

Second Left: The conservatory in the main house affords spectacular views of the evening sky.
Photograph by Rare Brick

Third Left: The Carriage House offers guests luxury and comfort in their choice of three well-appointed two-room suites.
Photograph by Rare Brick

Bottom Left: After a long day of work or play, guests return to the inn and relax in their private living room.
Photograph by Rare Brick

Facing Page: The historic inn is the epitome of urban elegance.
Photograph by Rare Brick

The Settlers Inn

Hawley, Pennsylvania

The Roaring '20s were coming to a close when the small community of Hawley, Pennsylvania, located in the scenic Lake Region of the Poconos Mountains, voted to build a hotel to promote tourism in their picturesque mountain town. Continuously revitalized and updated, The Settlers Inn—a charming 21-guestroom English-style Arts-and-Crafts hotel—delightfully harkens the architecture of that idealistic time in America's history. Artfully decorated with Mission-style furniture and Arts-and-Crafts touches, this small Pennsylvania hotel welcomes its guests to an abundance of life's quiet joys.

Although it had not been used as a hotel for quite some time when Grant and Jean Genzlinger discovered the inn, upon purchasing it in 1980, they made it their two-year mission to return it to the place of grandeur and respite of its past. Because of the inn's location on beautiful, peaceful grounds replete with lush greenery, a meandering stream and walking trail, the couple saw possibilities including a special and unique destination for weddings and retreats. The couple has married their individual talents—she, the inn coordinator and artful interior design mind behind the inn's well-appointed decor, and he, the executive chef of the inn's renowned farm-to-market restaurant, Chestnut Tavern—making The Settlers Inn a top Poconos inn.

While absorbing the lovely ambience—dining alfresco or by the inn's roaring fireplace—guests feast on The Settlers Inn's ever-changing menu, which reflects the best of the season, including fresh herbs from the property's own extensive gardens, along with some first-rate staples including fresh-baked artisan breads and an extensive wine list that has earned the inn an Award of Excellence from *Wine Spectator* magazine. Boasting an equal draw of activities that guests seek throughout each season—swimming, hiking, snow skiing, boating, antiquing or even taking a cooking class—the welcoming town of Hawley and natural beauty of the Poconos Mountains make for an event-filled stay.

Top Left: The inn is a gathering place for friends and family.
Photograph by Rare Brick

Second Left: Each of the 21 guestrooms is thoughtfully appointed with comfort foremost in mind.
Photograph by Rare Brick

Third Left: In winter, guests bask in the warmth of bluestone fireplaces.
Photograph by Rare Brick

Bottom Left: The inn's farm-to-table restaurant features a menu of delectable entrées that change seasonally.
Photograph by Rare Brick

Facing Page: The restored Arts-and-Crafts inn beckons guests to relax, play and rejuvenate.
Photograph by Rare Brick

Stone Hill Inn

Stowe, Vermont

As hospitality industry professionals, Amy and Hap Jordan saw an uncharted niche of the profession that caught their interest. With entrepreneurs' instincts, the couple wanted to build a luxurious getaway that focused on the intimacy of couples instead of appealing to families. Thus, the Stone Hill Inn was born in 1998, built from the ground up.

The historic village of Stowe, Vermont—first chartered in 1763—is the perfect backdrop for the charming, Shingle-style Stone Hill Inn. Known for its eclectic mix of entertainment, from Bavarian festivals to ideal skiing conditions, Stowe is a town that allows the inn's guests to be as active or leisurely as they would like. Visitors have a laundry list of activities to choose from, including outdoor concerts, fine art galleries, boutique shopping, hiking, tobogganing, canoeing and dog sledding. For those who choose not to venture out of the warm luxury of the inn, each room offers a Jacuzzi, fireplace and Pima cotton sheets, plus a billiards table or movie library for evening entertainment.

Hap's previous experience as a chef and Amy's long résumé of hotel and restaurant work has resulted in an upscale bed-and-breakfast inn with a strong emphasis on delicious breakfasts, served by candlelight at tables set for two. Three choices are offered each morning—perhaps peaches-and-cream-stuffed French toast, Canadian bacon and leek quiche or gingerbread pancakes—with famous Vermont maple syrup, of course. Stowe is home to more than 40 restaurants, and the concierge can make guests' dinner arrangements as well as help plan each day's excursions. Options include a fondue dinner and snowshoe tour, a water and wine canoe trip and winery tour, and the experience of being a chocolatier for a day.

With views pulled straight from a Robert Frost poem, nearby Mount Mansfield, the Worcester Mountains and Stone Hill Inn's perennial gardens induce a pervasive sense of calm. The peaceful, private setting makes the inn feel more like an exclusive estate and aided in earning it a spot as one of Forbes.com's 12 Best Bed-and-Breakfasts in North America.

Top Left: The exquisite guestrooms feature fireside Jacuzzis for two and other indulgent amenities to spoil visitors. It is the perfect place to celebrate a special occasion.
Photograph by Jumping Rocks Photography

Second Left: The living room is a cozy gathering place for cocktails, cards or watching flames dance on a cold winter evening.
Photograph by Glenn Moody

Bottom Left: An ideal spot for après-ski or after-dinner relaxation, the game room features a billiard table in front of the massive stone fireplace.
Photograph by Jumping Rocks Photography

Facing Page: Stone Hill Inn serves a different hors d'oeuvre to welcome guests each evening. Tonight—Savory Artichoke Cheesecake.
Photograph by Jumping Rocks Photography

Sugar Hill Inn

Sugar Hill, New Hampshire

When Steve Allen purchased Sugar Hill Inn he had a vision of recreating the classic New England Country Inn updated for the next generation.

Sugar Hill Inn began as a small farmhouse, built in 1789. Steve and assistant innkeeper Theresa Spear are building on the inn's 80-year-old tradition of hospitality, while sharing the good life with guests from around the world.

Steve, a graduate of the French Culinary Institute in Manhattan, with a keen interest in culinary travel, has focused on elevating the inn's cuisine and wine offerings. Today Chef Van Fortin's dishes are described quite simply as delicious works of art.

Original artwork, crafts, books, natural materials and fresh flowers are all part of the inn's focus on creating the perfect guest environment. The tavern room, replete with woodburning fireplace and cozy bar, brings guests together to meet and share the day's adventure. A new pool with waterfall invites relaxation and is carefully angled to capture magnificent vistas. A brand new cottage boasts cathedral ceilings, a stone fireplace, wide plank floors, French doors, a whirlpool and sauna, natural slate tile and a marble vanity as well as a flat-screen television and Bose sound system, making it the ultimate in luxury and romance.

For Theresa, hospitality is more then just good service; it is about connection. She loves helping guests plan hikes or other adventures and surprise their partners with champagne and chocolates. The beautiful gardens reflect Theresa's sense of style and appreciation of nature.

Located at the northern end of the Franconia Notch, Sugar Hill is the ideal location from which to explore the White Mountains of New Hampshire, an area known for winter sports, summer hiking and fall foliage.

Top Left: Each dinner and dessert is a work of art.
Photograph by Jumping Rocks Photography

Second Left: The Peckett Suite is the epitome of luxurious relaxation.
Photograph by Jumping Rocks Photography

Bottom Left: Guests savor breakfast while gazing at the natural environment that envelops the inn.
Photograph by Jumping Rocks Photography

Facing Page: Panoramic views of Mount Lafayette are particularly impressive during the winter months.
Photograph by Jumping Rocks Photography

Tara—A Country Inn

Clark, Pennsylvania

*O*wners Donna and Jim Winner considered themselves unbelievably fortunate when they purchased the abandoned former home of Charles Koonce—a United States senator who had made his fortune in coal and real estate in the 19th century—at a public auction. As luck would have it, the majestic Antebellum Greek Revival located in Clark, Pennsylvania, bore striking similarities to *Gone With the Wind*'s Tara; Donna and Jim just happened to be passionate historians of the beloved American novel.

The acquisition had concluded a two-year long search for the site of the perfect inn. Already quite seasoned in the hospitality industry, the couple had started in the business in 1979 when they purchased the Shenango Inn, a 72-room Colonial hotel in the residential section of Sharon, Pennsylvania. Longing to have more face-to-face interaction and personalized service, Donna and Jim concluded their countrywide search, ironically, in their own backyard. They held high expectations, all of which they could envision—after some hard work, of course—in the Clark property.

Hard work is not something that had ever discouraged the Winners. Jim and Donna both began life on simple Mercer County, Pennsylvania, dairy farms. Their modest upbringings taught them the power of hard work, integrity, commitment and most importantly, the value of altruism. With the creation of The Club®, the automotive anti-theft device, Jim Winner created a successful business and has aggressively launched a campaign to bring more jobs and better quality of life to the residents of his native Mercer County. Winner International, Winner Steel, Winner Aviation, The Winner department store, and other hotel and banquet venues have been among Jim and Donna's contributions to Shenango Valley's industrial, tourism and hospitality economies, as well as the 800 jobs they have created in the steel-depressed area.

Top Left: Fairy-tale weddings are a trademark of this spectacular inn. The gazebo, formal gardens and Antebellum backdrop offer the perfect setting for a couple's special day.
Photograph by Paul Witkowski

Bottom Left: Rich with *Gone With the Wind* memorabilia, Civil War collections and exquisite antiques, Tara is a virtual museum enjoyed by overnight, dinner and tour guests alike.
Photograph by Richard Smaltz Photography

Facing Page: Ashley's Gourmet Dining Room is the elegant setting of a delectable seven-course experience. The memory-making, candlelit ambience is enhanced through the talents of the pianist and white-glove service of the tuxedo-clad waitstaff.
Photograph by Gregory Barringer, Pro Images of PA

In June 1986, after two years of careful and appropriate restoration, they unveiled Tara–A Country Inn and opened the inn with their personal collection of fine antiques. With an interior that feels at once elegant, expansive and comfortable, Tara's beautiful heritage has been restored, preserved and celebrated. Donna and Jim have devoted years to Tara's transformation, making it into one of the premier inns in the country. After two additions, Tara now has 27 beautiful guestrooms.

Ashley's Gourmet Dining Room, Stonewall's Tavern and the Old South Armory Restaurant offer gourmet meals and tea-time feasts. Staff at the inn even wear period costumes, adding authenticity to the experience. Banquet facilities, indoor and outdoor pools, public tours and elegant gardens have made Tara a household name in the tri-state area surrounding Mercer County. Tara also hosts fine dining for guests of the Winners' other remarkable inn, Buhl Mansion Guesthouse & Spa, with weekend shuttle service between the two properties.

Due to its location, fine cuisine and ability to accommodate many guests and large parties, over the last two decades, the western Pennsylvania inn has become a sought-after spot for destination weddings. Many brides have depended on the inn to host the wedding of their dreams—they have not been disappointed, as thousands of storybook weddings have taken place in the incredible formal gardens. Upon arrival, a picturesque setting readies guests for something special—be it a few days of romance, a memorable corporate retreat, a golfing vacation or even a restful mini-vacation—Tara casts a spell of romance and quaint warmth. Guests may first visit the inn based on its reputation, but Tara's high rate of repeat guests offers undeniable proof that it consistently exceeds all expectations.

Above: Inspired by one of the greatest novels and movies of all time, Tara is devoted to guests who expect the exceptional and appreciate the best.
Photograph by Gregory Barringer, Pro Images of PA

Facing Page Top Left: Guests take pleasure in one of the 27 *Gone With the Wind*, Civil War-themed rooms boasting Jacuzzis, sunken tubs, fireplaces and gracious sitting areas.
Photograph by Richard Smaltz Photography

Facing Page Top Right: Rhett's Room, as distinguished and stately as the movie legend himself, welcomes guests with a roaring fire, grand furnishings, complementary bottle of champagne and delicious treats.
Photograph by Gregory Barringer, Pro Images of PA

Facing Page Bottom: Belle's Boudoir is a bit naughty, decorated in red, gold and cream to give a very rich effect with a floor-to-ceiling canopy bed.
Photograph by Jon Lisbon, Photografis

Above: Coombs Inn, page 170

Southeastern U.S.

Chapter Four

Antrim 1844 Country Inn

Taneytown, Maryland

*R*ecapture a time long lost when grace, elegance and hospitality were the bastion of great hotels. Richard and Dort Mollett applied their expertise to restore this pre-Civil War plantation along with its original Ice House, Carriage House and pertinent outbuildings, situated on 25 manicured acres. The formal gardens, which often serve as a spectacular wedding site, were recreated from historical documents. After a year of masterful renovations, Antrim 1844 Country Inn opened with four breathtaking guestrooms in 1988.

Today, the inn consists of more than 40 guestrooms, is run by a staff of over 100 employees—led by general manager John Vonnes—and is acclaimed for its superb cuisine and romantic accommodations. Each room at Antrim is filled with exquisite comfort and elegance among its feather duvets, monogrammed robes, oil paintings, and oriental rugs—all of which embrace the ambience of Antebellum grace with European style.

Guests may enjoy afternoon tea in the drawing rooms while the music from the grand piano gracefully fills the mansion as evening hors d'oeuvres are served. One of the more defining qualities of Antrim is its morning continental breakfast delivery. The breakfast staff tiptoes to each guestroom and sets a tray filled with muffins, fruit, coffee and a newspaper outside each door. A full breakfast is served on the veranda a short time later.

Wanting to couple superb lodging with a fine-dining experience, the Molletts opened Antrim's internationally acclaimed Smokehouse Restaurant in the early 1990s. Sommelier/maître d' hôtel Sia Ayrom manages the seven dining rooms while executive chef Michael Gettier masterfully creates the menu for the restaurant that has won DiRoNA and *Wine Spectator* awards for the last decade. Guests are invited to discover the genteel spirit of 19th-century America while their needs are anticipated, met and exceeded.

Top Left: A proud member of the National Historic Trust of America, the 1844-built mansion is a classic example of Greek Revival architecture with Federal influences.
Photograph by George Gardner

Second Left: The south drawing room—the perfect place to enjoy afternoon tea and a good book—features white marble fireplaces hand-carved by sculptor William Rinehart.
Photograph by George Gardner

Third Left: After a day of touring Gettysburg, which is just 12 miles away, antiquing or hiking in the Catoctin Mountains, those who stay in the well-appointed Ulysses S. Grant Suite can relax in the double Jacuzzi while sipping champagne.
Photograph by George Gardner

Bottom Left: Housing more than 17,000 bottles of fine wine, the internationally acclaimed cellar offers private tastings as well as delectable evening cuisine.
Photograph by Tim Edwards

Facing Page: Romance fills the beautifully manicured formal gardens as guests linger by the bronze fountains at sunset.
Photograph by Christian Oth Studios

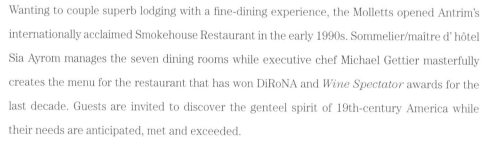

The Ashby Inn & Restaurant

Paris, Virginia

When guests arrive at The Ashby Inn & Restaurant, there is an irresistible desire to walk lighter and breathe deeper. Rolling hills surround this inn that is situated on three beautifully landscaped acres and also backs up to a vast conservancy of 3,000 acres. Not only can guests soak in the beauty of the Blue Ridge Mountains, they can also easily embark on a trip along the Appalachian Trail. With 10 rooms divided between two separate buildings, The Ashby Inn has enough space to accommodate guests without losing its intimate ambience and excellent personal service. Its location among horse farms and more than 20 wineries makes this inn an excellent place to enjoy a glass of wine and revisit a slower pace of life.

With more than two decades of outstanding service, the inn's quaint charm inspired Jackie and Chuck Leopold to purchase it in October 2005. Between the Main House and the School House, there are plenty of luxurious options. The School House, originally Paris' one-room educational site, was converted by John and Roma Sherman, the original owners, and now contains four junior suites replete with every imaginable comfort, mountain-view balconies and woodburning fireplaces. The Main House, more historical in style, also offers rooms with endless amenities. The Ashby's guests enjoy locally made selections—including chocolates from the nearby chocolatier at the nightly turn-down service.

One of the main perks at the inn is its highly acclaimed restaurant, with cuisine from delectable crab cakes and hand-cut steaks to scrumptious desserts. Chef Frank Mayo takes great pride in preparing menus that complement each season. The restaurant's four dining rooms are stunning as well with a pine wood floor entrance, library with fireplace and a stone terrace that provides breathtaking views of the conservancy land. After staying at The Ashby, guests discover a certain, indescribable magic. With unparalleled cuisine, impeccable accommodations and service, guests come back often to escape the everyday and experience the extraordinary.

Top Left: Breathtaking views of the rolling hills and the Blue Ridge Mountains invite guests to relax in the Adirondack chairs.
Photograph by George Gardner

Second Left: Sweet greens and welcoming coral hues define one of the lovely guestrooms in the Main House.
Photograph by George Gardner

Third Left: A winding, wooden fence gives definition to the lush, picturesque grounds of the inn.
Photograph by George Gardner

Bottom Left: Chef Frank Mayo oversees all culinary details, adjusting menus to reflect both the season and personal artistry.
Photograph by George Gardner

Facing Page: With white walls, dark shutters and humble columns, one glance of the Main House at The Ashby Inn conveys its Americana charm.
Photograph by George Gardner

Beechwood Inn

Clayton, Georgia

*M*ention a romantic wine country inn, and images of Napa, Sonoma and Tuscany come to mind. One likely would not envision a quiet, intimate retreat dedicated to savoring the grape in northern Georgia's Blue Ridge Mountains; yet David and Gayle Darugh's Beechwood Inn is just that. Nestled among wildflowers, herb gardens and indigenous foliage alive with color throughout the year, the award-winning bed-and-breakfast affords guests luxury accommodations, gourmet dining and an enviable wine selection in an idyllic setting.

Rabun County, the inn's home, is a nature enthusiast's dream, offering ample opportunities for rafting, canoeing, mountain biking, hiking, fly-fishing and hunting. For those desiring more urbane activities, the area offers several championship golf courses, as well as museums, arts events and antiques. Perhaps most intriguing are the local vineyards, which host tours and tastings, forging the way for a region of prolific producers. Georgia's relatively recent entrée into the winemaking market impelled the Darughs to purchase Beechwood Inn in 2000, and the couple has since worked to promote the area's fine varietals as well as exquisite appellations from around the world. Up to 16 guests can enjoy afternoon wine tastings on the front porch, prix fixe meals replete with perfect pairings in the intimate *Wine Spectator* Award of Excellence-winning dining room and frequent winemaker dinners.

Beechwood proves to be the ideal setting for romantic couples' getaways. Indeed, the inn was voted Number One Inn for a Weekend Getaway by *Inn Traveler* magazine for two consecutive years. David and Gayle's fervent passion for wine—both were raised among the vineyards in Napa Valley and have taught wine appreciation courses, and Gayle has served as national president of the American Wine Society—as well as locally grown products, which pepper the menu, infuses the inn with a convivial atmosphere and local flavor. They invite people to step out of their frenetic lives and recharge at Beechwood—with a loved one, a good book and of course, a glass of Georgia's finest.

Top Left: Red summer impatiens highlight the appeal of the Beechwood Inn, giving the house a rich color scheme.
Photograph by David G. Darugh

Second Left: Beechwood guests enjoy "wine-thirty" everyday between 5:30 and 6:30 p.m.—a flavorful treat for the early evening.
Photograph by David G. Darugh

Third Left: Among others, the Savannah Suite offers working fireplaces that entice guests to stay in for the evening.
Photograph by David G. Darugh

Bottom Left: Visitors often relax on the treetop front porch, a guest favorite.
Photograph by David G. Darugh

Facing Page: As an additional bonus to the hospitality at Beechwood Inn, the bed-and-breakfast bottles its own wine—a perfect souvenir.
Photograph by David G. Darugh

Chanticleer Inn

Lookout Mountain, Georgia

S et atop Lookout Mountain, Chanticleer Inn offers guests many comforts of a smaller English country inn. Peacefulness prevails in the quiet setting of stone cottages sitting among mature hemlock, oak and magnolia trees. A variety of shrubs and flowers in season enhance the grounds and walkways.

Each room offers its own bath, heating and cooling system and luxurious Kingsdown mattress, and includes many antiques and botanical prints from Trowbridge Galleries of London. Some rooms come with Jacuzzi tubs, steam showers and gas-log fireplaces. A delicious homemade breakfast is prepared by a graduate of the esteemed Johnson & Wales College of Culinary Arts. During breakfast, guests may take pleasure in observing a variety of feeding birds—woodpeckers, cardinals, finches, wrens and titmice, among others.

Activities of the day may include enjoying the fascinating rock formations and views of Rock City Gardens located down the street, as well as nearby historic battlefields such as Chickamauga, Lookout Mountain and Missionary Ridge.

In 2001, when Chris and Susan Maclellan purchased Chanticleer Inn, it was in a state of sad disarray. The Maclellans went to work restoring the vintage inn, which first began its modest operations in the early 1930s. By refinishing floors, making structural repairs, installing new heating and cooling systems and redecorating throughout, the inn came forth with a bold and appealing character.

Top Left: Guests enjoy reading or visiting by the fireplace in the common living room, which is appointed with comfortable furnishings.
Photograph by George Gardner

Second Left: The pool area is inviting and conveniently accessed from the guestrooms.
Photograph by George Gardner

Third Left: This living room is located within one of the guest quarters.
Photograph by George Gardner

Bottom Left: The courtyard is replete with a bubbling fountain, blooming plants and seating area.
Photograph by George Gardner

Facing Page: The patio leads to the reception area.
Photograph by George Gardner

Susan's parents, Judy and Kirby Wahl, became the innkeepers upon the inn's reopening for business. The Wahls have traveled extensively, visiting numerous inns in America and various other countries of the world. They are very helpful in assisting guests with their itinerary of sightseeing, restaurants to visit and things to do.

While life might not offer endless hours of tranquility, Chanticleer Inn provides guests with many luxuries, great cuisine and purifying natural environmental gifts that restore and elevate the human spirit, as witnessed by the frequency of returning guests to this garden spot located in the beautiful and appealing Chattanooga area.

Above: Azaleas line the pathway to the inn's gracious entrance.
Photograph by George Gardner

Right: Arched, leaded windows enhance the porch dining area.
Photograph by George Gardner

Facing Page Top: Antique botanical prints from Trowbridge Galleries hang above the queen-sized bed.
Photograph by George Gardner

Facing Page Bottom: A favorite for romantic weekends, the room has a king-sized bed, gas-log fireplace, sitting area and Jacuzzi tub.
Photograph by George Gardner

Coombs Inn

Apalachicola, Florida

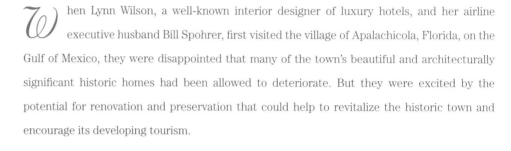

When Lynn Wilson, a well-known interior designer of luxury hotels, and her airline executive husband Bill Spohrer, first visited the village of Apalachicola, Florida, on the Gulf of Mexico, they were disappointed that many of the town's beautiful and architecturally significant historic homes had been allowed to deteriorate. But they were excited by the potential for renovation and preservation that could help to revitalize the historic town and encourage its developing tourism.

Apalachicola had been a wealthy cotton port until the Civil War when the Union Navy established a blockade that prevented the export of cotton. After the war, the economy recovered based on timber, sponge fishing and seafood, which financed the construction of dozens of elaborate Victorian mansions.

Notable among them was the home of James N. Coombs described by *The Apalachicola Times* as "the most elegant house in town." James Coombs was considered to be the wealthiest man in Apalachicola. He owned sawmills, the bank and a lumber company, which shipped worldwide. He built his luxurious new home in 1905 to give his growing family a larger residence that would reflect their social and economic status.

Lynn Wilson, who had renovated such historic buildings as the Biltmore Hotel in Coral Gables, Florida; the DuPont Hotel in Wilmington, Delaware; and Queen Elizabeth's former home in Ascot, England, was fascinated by the potential of Apalachicola and especially of the Coombs house. She envisioned the town becoming the historic centerpiece of a new northern Florida tourist area already known for its pristine white beaches, fishing and boating and lush national forests. She was not disappointed.

Top Left: Tranquil vistas of the broad Apalachicola River and bay are an easy stroll from the inn.
Photograph by Debbie Hooper

Second Left: Spacious verandas and private porches are comfortable areas for guests to relax or catch up on some reading.
Photograph by Brian Gassel

Third Left: Camillia Gardens, Hall and Gazebo are the perfect venue for weddings and receptions.
Photograph by Debbie Hooper

Bottom Left: Morning coffee or afternoon teas are delightful in the peaceful gardens and verandas.
Photograph by Brian Gassel

Facing Page: The Coombs Victorian Mansion, built in 1904 and located in the picturesque historic district, is beautifully adorned with fine antiques, original 19th-century oil paintings, crystal chandeliers, 17 fireplaces and 23 luxurious guest suites.
Photograph by Debbie Hooper

The Spohrers bought the abandoned Coombs house and converted the old mansion into a beautiful and comfortable inn. Luxury bathrooms were added for each room, a modern breakfast kitchen was installed, and the house, named the Coombs Mansion, was painted a cheery sunshine yellow. Lynn furnished the mansion with antiques and original paintings, many from her own collection.

The Coombs Mansion was so popular that a neighboring Victorian mansion was soon purchased and renovated. The new accommodations, Coombs Villas, are set in the midst of a garden with a gazebo, copies of classic statues and a meeting hall converted from a carriage house.

A third Victorian building, called Coombs Veranda Suites, was added recently. It features four beautifully furnished suites which provide the most luxurious accommodations for discerning guests. The Coombs Inn now has 23 elegant suites, of which seven offer romantic Jacuzzi baths and 17 boast original fireplaces. All rooms have in-room coffee makers, guest robes, cable television and wireless access.

The inn offers gourmet breakfasts and wine receptions on Friday and Saturday evenings. Beach-going guests may use the inn's beach chairs and umbrellas. Others may prefer to check out bicycles to tour the historic district. Guests are also invited once a month for high tea at the nearby historic home of the owners of Coombs Inn, Lady Lynn and Sir William Spohrer. Sir William was honored to have been named a Knight of the Order of the Lion of Finland by the president of Finland.

Above: Heaven Eleven is enhanced with an English Tudor hand-carved four-poster bed, a Jacuzzi for two, bath suite with his-and-hers pedestal sinks, personal bidet, separate walk-in shower, champagne refrigerator and an antique boudoir dressing table—all concealed behind French double-beveled, stained glass doors. Heaven Eleven is flawlessly appointed for a romantic bridal or anniversary retreat.
Photograph by Brian Gassel

Facing Page Top Left: The yellow-hued dining room is decorated with English floral chintz and mahogany Chippendale chairs and hosts gourmet breakfasts, teas and wine receptions.
Photograph by Brian Gassel

Facing Page Top Right: The rich cypress paneling of the lobby glistens with the soft glow of an occasional evening fire in one of Coomb's Inn's 17 decorative fireplaces.
Photograph by Brian Gassel

Facing Page Bottom Left: Veranda Suite A offers guests a beautiful living room and fireplace suite that sleeps an additional guest in the two double beds within the adjacent sleeping suite.
Photograph by Brian Gassel

Facing Page Bottom Right: The sophistication of this guestroom carries through to a cozy, serene sitting room.
Photograph by Brian Gassel

Elizabeth Pointe Lodge

Amelia Island, Florida

With the warm sun glimmering and the crisp ocean air filling each breath, guests can enter a retreat where having no agenda is the norm. Elizabeth Pointe Lodge's Nantucket-style Main House contains 20 guestrooms and was built to allow guests from the northeast to reminisce and spark curiosity in those from the southeast; it provides a truly coastal experience. The adjacent Ocean House has king-sized beds floating in the middle of its two large suites, and Miller Cottage is perfect for families with its galley kitchen and ocean deck.

Thirteen miles of beach follow the length of the island where David and Susan Caples chose to build the lodge in 1992. Because it is only one and a half miles wide, the island offers a perfect escape for those needing to forget their cares. Occasionally, guests can even walk onto the beach and find it completely vacant.

Among its many indulgences, Elizabeth Pointe Lodge's staff is available 24 hours a day. If guests have a long drive and will not arrive until late in the evening, the staff will be waiting to meet any and all requests, including kitchen service. When guests wake up in the morning, they will find a newspaper outside their door along with a *New York Times Digest*. A fully tended breakfast buffet offers both hot and cold options for a three-hour window each morning, allowing guests to come down at their leisure. While there is a wine hour every afternoon, beverages and fresh cookies are available at any time throughout the day. The inn is not only equipped with Wi-Fi, but it also has computers and other business services available.

Whether guests have come to the seaside to spend a day writing in a journal or playing a round of golf at one of Amelia Island's six golf courses, Elizabeth Pointe Lodge offers everything they could desire at the end of each day.

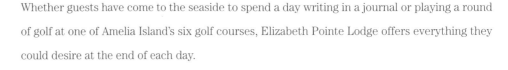

Top Left: The Elizabeth Pointe compound has three guest buildings just on the other side of the dunes.
Photograph by Clyde Wilkes

Second Left: Each guestroom has its own character, and more than half have ocean views.
Photograph by Jan Johannes

Third Left: This gathering place boasts hundreds of books and nautical artifacts. On cool winter nights the woodburning fireplace roars.
Photograph by Jan Johannes

Bottom Left: With a staff intent on making every moment special, guests are afforded a generous array of breakfast options as they enjoy 180-degree seaside views.
Photograph by Jan Johannes

Facing Page: The grey and white Nantucket Shingle-style inn has a commanding presence on its beachfront location.
Photograph by Jan Johannes

Gideon Ridge Inn

Blowing Rock, North Carolina

For a relaxing getaway in a one-of-a-kind tranquil setting, inn enthusiasts need look no further than Gideon Ridge Inn. Set on a five-acre ridge at nearly 4,000 feet above sea level overlooking the Blue Ridge Mountains, Gideon Ridge is an elegant stone house in a historic district offering nearly panoramic views up to 90 miles on clear days.

With the Blue Ridge Parkway just a mile and a half away, ample opportunities exist for guests to engage in hiking, sightseeing and myriad other outdoor activities. The quaint town of Blowing Rock, North Carolina, is home to delightful shops, restaurants and a park, which often hosts enticing recreational events. In spite of the nearby inviting attractions, guests might find themselves reluctant to leave the placid ambience that permeates Gideon Ridge.

From the library with its chestnut-beamed ceilings, oil paintings and original art to the Old World billiard room, inviting nooks abound at every turn. Enchanting outdoor leisure exists on the home's broad stone terraces, which are adorned with wicker furniture and plush pillows. The outdoor gardens are a favorite place to walk amongst the wildflowers, sit and listen to the birds or simply drink in the serene, wooded mountaintop setting.

Innkeepers Cindy and Cobb Milner have been at Gideon Ridge since 1990, and under their guidance the cuisine has been elevated to fine-dining status. Guests enjoy cocktails and hors d'oeuvres in the library every evening and can enjoy dinner at Restaurant G, specializing in steak and seafood prepared in the classic style. The menu changes weekly, reflecting the freshest organic ingredients that can be found in the area.

Set in a secluded, relaxing locale with nearby attractions, Gideon Ridge Inn is an idyllic retreat certain to satisfy.

Top Left: The inn is open year-round; guests love the winter season and the occasional snow.
Photograph by C. Milner

Second Left: A fireplace and private porch with majestic views are features of the old master bedroom.
Photograph by C. Milner

Third Left: Traditional European cuisine meets the classic American steakhouse at Restaurant G.
Photograph by C. Milner

Bottom Left: Cool breezes sail through the covered stone terrace.
Photograph by C. Milner

Facing Page: Autumn sunrises overlooking Blackberry Gorge are beyond breathtaking.
Photograph by C. Milner

The Hamilton-Turner Inn

Savannah, Georgia

*U*pon visiting Savannah, Georgia, one can clearly see why Sherman elected to spare this Southern city during the Civil War, famously "giving" it to President Lincoln as a Christmas gift. Upon burning everything in his march to the sea, even Sherman could not bear to destroy the majestic old city with its spectacular mid-18th-century architecture and lush flora.

Founded in 1733 as the first master-planned city in the United States, Savannah still retains almost all of its originally planned city squares. The great Southern lady that she is, Savannah has gracefully risen above the Civil War, two major citywide fires, modern-age growing pains as well as bits of scandal and gossip, which in truth has only made her stronger and more beguiling. The fifth most popular destination in the United States, with typical Southern hospitality Savannah beckons all age groups to experience life in this historic piece of the country—from City Market to the delicious eeriness of its storied cemeteries.

At the center of the Historic District, in Lafayette Square, is the renowned Hamilton-Turner Inn, the most photographed home in Savannah. The expansive park-side mansion was built in 1873 by alderman and successful businessman Samuel Pugh Hamilton for his family and later sold to Dr. Francis Turner in 1915. Having been once saved from demolition, the Hamilton-Turner House operated as an apartment building for nearly 30 years. The home gained attention under the management of Joe Odom, whose notorious parties were made famous in the John Berendt book *Midnight in the Garden of Good and Evil*.

Converted into a bed-and-breakfast in 1997, present owners Gay and Jim Dunlop take most auspiciously the task of continuing the great legacy of this fine historic building by maintaining

Top Left: The General Nathaniel Greene Suite 302 is a stately room, boasting airy 12-foot ceilings, a claw-foot soaking bath and an antique queen-sized bed.
Photograph by Roi Crapse

Second Left: The spacious John Wesley Suite 404 features treetop views of Lafayette Square, two four-poster queen-sized beds and a double whirlpool spa bath.
Photograph by Roi Crapse

Third Left: Guests drink in 11-foot views of the park in the luxurious James Oglethorpe Suite 304. This suite offers an antique queen-sized bed, double whirlpool spa bath and a working fireplace.
Photograph by Roi Crapse

Bottom Left: The light-filled Johnny Mercer Room 202 has a four-poster queen-sized bed, bay window seating area and a claw-foot soaking bath.
Photograph by Roi Crapse

Facing Page: Stately elegance defines the Second Empire Mansion on Lafayette Square in the center of Savannah's historic district.
Photograph by David Strohl

and upgrading it. A gracious aura surrounds the exterior of the inn as well as the interior, whose immaculate and handsomely appointed appearance is breathtaking. Original heart pine flooring, splendid chandeliers, floor-to-ceiling windows and intricate woodwork set the ambience of the inn. Its décor has been perfected to the last detail, at once making guests feel welcomed and awed by its historic grandeur. Seventeen luxurious guestrooms and suites have been designed to appear diverse, yet encompass elegance and sophistication. Traditionally furnished with antiques and modern-day amenities, rooms include fireplaces, whirlpool spa baths or claw-foot soaking tubs, the highest quality room and bath linens, as well as spa therapy bath toiletries. Modern amenities such as televisions, DVD players and wireless internet connections in every room ensure that guests are comforted by their links to home or the office. In addition to the main house, the original carriage house includes three guestrooms and is the perfect site for a ladies' weekend or multi-generational family quarters.

A delectable Southern breakfast, changing daily, greets guests every morning while they dine surrounded by the beauty of the gardens. A guest's days are filled with tours, fine dining and quiet strolls all arranged by concierge services available for every detail from arrival to departure. After a busy day of touring, guests can retire to the mansion for an afternoon of iced tea and sweets in the parlor or early evening wine and hors d'oeuvres before an unforgettable night on the town. With nightly turndown service and cookies at each bedside, the pampering does not end until guests close their eyes for the night.

As long-time innkeepers, Jim and Gay have invested their experience and wisdom into restoring The Hamilton-Turner Inn to its original grandeur as the Grand Victorian Lady. Judging by their high rate of repeat guests from families to business people, and media exposure, they have happily succeeded.

Above: The spirited Noble Jones Suite 301 offers soaring 12-foot ceilings, a romantic king-sized canopy bed, working fireplace and a double whirlpool spa bath.
Photograph by Roi Crapse

Facing Page Top: A sumptuous gourmet Southern breakfast is served each morning in the formal dining room, overlooking the park.
Photograph by Roi Crapse

Facing Page Bottom: The elegant yet comfortable parlor is a great place to relax with an early morning coffee, for afternoon refreshments or during wine and hors d'oeuvres service.
Photograph by Roi Crapse

Inn at Riverbend

Pearisburg, Virginia

estled high on a bluff in Pearisburg, Virginia, Inn at Riverbend greets arriving guests with its overwhelming 180-degree panoramic view of the mountains and the New River. Built in 2003 by owners Lynn and Linda Hayes, the inn is graced with 200 feet of decks and terraces, where all seven rooms open to the sloping green hills and vibrant river waters.

Designed with a contemporary Southern style, with metal roofing and white railing, the inn appeals to guests of all varieties. Since opening, the inn has attracted visitors from 42 states and 10 countries, including England, Germany, South Africa and China. From couples needing to reconnect to fishing partners who have come for hours of reeling in trout, this is a place where guests are welcomed like old friends.

A typical day varies for guests of the inn, but what matters most is finding time to release any worries and breathe in the beauty of the New River Valley. After a satisfying breakfast of fruits, breads and the hot entrée of the day, visitors can venture into the outdoors and take a hike on the Appalachian Trail, enjoy a canoe trip down the United States' oldest river or simply jump back in bed and catch up on some sleep. The goal of Inn at Riverbend is to meet every need of its guests and exceed their expectations.

Because it sits in the midst of two migratory bird paths, the inn is surrounded by the gentle whispers of traveling birds. During this time, explorers might see hummingbirds, golden finches, indigo buntings, orioles and more. Many of these birds fly to Costa Rica and Mexico and then return back to the New River Valley the next year. Whether guests are looking for a place to fish for small mouth bass or a romantic escape from everyday life to rest in the sway of a hammock, the inn is a destination to visit again and again.

Top Left: Guests often enjoy a favorite book and a glass of wine in front of the fireplace.
Photograph by George Gardner

Second Left: The abundant windows within guestrooms offer a great morning view of the mountains and the rising mist over the New River.
Photograph by George Gardner

Third Left: Breakfast on the entry-level deck of the great room overlooks the New River and the mountains.
Photograph by George Gardner

Bottom Left: The owner loves fly-fishing on the New River with Jackson, one of the inn dogs.
Photograph by George Gardner

Facing Page: Relaxing in the hammock—under the trees and by the pond—affords a view of the birds, mountains and the rear of Inn at Riverbend.
Photograph by George Gardner

Middleton Inn

Washington, Virginia

"*A* class act" is how *Condé Nast Traveller* magazine recently described Middleton Inn, as a historic country estate "with authentic Virginia taste and quality."

The elegant bed-and-breakfast inn, with its acres of scenic horse paddocks, graces the historic district of Washington, Virginia, a charming village originally laid out by George Washington. Middleton Inn is a short stroll from the world-renowned restaurant the Inn at Little Washington, less than a dozen miles from the beautiful Shenandoah National Park and 67 miles west of the nation's capital.

Built in 1840 by Middleton Miller, the same man who designed and manufactured the Confederate uniform in the Civil War, the deep past of Middleton Inn appears in every detail. The estate features a Federal manor house with its original architecture preserved; four exquisitely appointed rooms with private marble baths; a restored guest cottage originally built in the mid-1800s by an apprentice of Thomas Jefferson; and a restored two-bedroom log house, built in the 1700s near the time George Washington surveyed the town and drank from the cabin's well.

Strolling the grounds of the estate, one can still see the original smoke house, the summer kitchen and what was once the slaves' quarters.

All of the lodging accommodations have working fireplaces, breathtaking views of the Blue Ridge Mountains and myriad luxuries and amenities—twice-daily maid service, evening turndown service, complementary afternoon wine, evening port and a three-course gourmet breakfast. The inn's porches provide a perfect setting for sipping wine after a day of hiking in the Shenandoah National Park, antiquing, touring Monticello or visiting nearby

Top Left: Belle and Shadow graze among the buttercups in one of the inn's paddocks.
Photograph by Jumping Rocks Photography

Second Left: The handsome Ascot Room, named after the famous horserace in England, features beautiful views of the Blue Ridge Mountains.
Photograph by Tom Bagley and Gail Greco

Third Left: Chef Jerry Goebel gathers organic vegetables for his scrumptious vegetarian and gruyère frittatas.
Photograph courtesy of Middleton Inn

Bottom Left: Proprietor Mary Ann Kuhn has two foxhounds, Prince Charles and Lady Carolina, as well as a lab, Hannah.
Photograph by Jumping Rocks Photography

Facing Page: Built in 1840, the inn has a commanding hilltop presence in the historic district of Washington, Virginia.
Photograph by Jumping Rocks Photography

wineries and vineyards. Evening port may be taken in front of a roaring fire in the drawing room before retiring to a bed of luxurious linens. Not to be missed are the inn's famous English scones served during a scrumptious three-course breakfast on Herend china in the dining room or on one of the porches, weather permitting. And for four-legged guests, the inn's special pampering includes homemade biscuits for those staying in its special pet-friendly accommodations.

Owned and operated by Mary Ann Kuhn, a former CBS News producer and *Washington Post* reporter, Middleton Inn has received the AAA four-diamond award for the past 10 years for "excellence in accommodations and service." It is the highest rated bed and breakfast by AAA in the mid-Atlantic.

Middleton Inn's setting offers a chance to trace the tapestry of history—all in the comfort of indulging hospitality and Southern gentility.

Top Right: Adirondack chairs beneath a flowering cherry tree await guests taking a stroll.
Photograph by Jumping Rocks Photography

Bottom Right: A two-person Jacuzzi soothes the body and soul after a day in the country visiting wineries, perusing antique shops or hiking in Shenandoah National Park.
Photograph by Jumping Rocks Photography

Facing Page Top: The elegant front foyer opens to breathtaking mountain views.
Photograph by Jumping Rocks Photography

Facing Page Bottom: Guests enjoy complimentary afternoon wine and cheese on the front porch—on sunny days, breakfast is served there as well.
Photograph by Jumping Rocks Photography

The Monteagle Inn

Monteagle, Tennessee

Every week for 25 years, Jim Harmon hopscotched the country, working for somebody, yet racking up the frequent flyer miles and hotel credits to take friends and family around the world, from Italy to Latvia and on to the Great Wall of China. But eventually, Jim had to work for himself—it is better for the soul.

Jim purchased The Monteagle Inn in 2002 after looking at dozens of inns in several Southern states. The search took almost a year. "My extensive travel," Jim says, "provided me with a myriad of opportunities to develop the perfect travel experience." The Monteagle Inn is that experience.

Operating the inn personally—along with an invaluable staff of five—Jim captured the essences of Italy and France, designing The Monteagle as a reminiscence of inns that he had experienced in Tuscany and Provence. Guests enter the property through a stone and brick driveway. Their first impression is the herb garden boarding the sidewalk that approaches the inn, where they enjoy the scents of a variety of herbs used by the chef in The Monteagle's daily cooking. Guests then see the smiling face of the innkeeper who opens the door for their arrival.

This brick and stucco exterior provides a hint of the Italian influence found throughout the inn. The impressive front porch is a popular place to relax and enjoy a glass of wine from the inn's extensive wine selection, while the patio and gardens also allow a fabulous setting for a peaceful and relaxing interlude.

Top Left: Six-hundred thread count linens and luxurious comfort help provide a wonderful night's sleep.
Photograph by Jumping Rocks Photography

Second Left: The inn's mountain gourmet breakfast—acclaimed by food critics—provides a beautiful start to the day.
Photograph by Jumping Rocks Photography

Third Left: Romantic and indulgent, wine is a perfect way to set the mood.
Photograph by Jumping Rocks Photography

Bottom Left: The inn has an extensive wine collection for guests' enjoyment.
Photograph by Jumping Rocks Photography

Facing Page: The Monteagle Inn says: "Escape to our treasure, treasure your escape."
Photograph by Jumping Rocks Photography

Along with these large social spaces and herb, flower and vegetable gardens, The Monteagle Inn anticipates and fulfills guests' every need. The spacious bedrooms have soft linens and oversized bathrooms and are designed with Tuscan art, antiques and oriental rugs. Wireless internet is also available.

The inn's mountain gourmet breakfast was acclaimed by *Southern Living* magazine to be "among the best we have ever experienced." The breakfast includes eggs béarnaise, herb-roasted sweet potato fries, broiled grapefruit and New Orleans praline French toast. Breakfast will never taste the same.

Located in the general vicinity of the University of the South, The Monteagle does draw its fair share of the school's supportive parents. But the locale makes the inn a prime target for Nashville and Chattanooga weekend getaways. The abundance of nature trails and waterfalls in the South Cumberland State Park system beckon nature lovers, especially in the fall as a last escape before winter. The Monteagle Inn truly becomes an exceptional gathering place for the remarkable individual celebrating a special moment in time.

Top Right: Guests may never want to leave such luxurious rooms—it is best to enjoy the moment.
Photograph by Jumping Rocks Photography

Bottom Right: Italian and French art and décor blend with mountain surroundings for a perfect setting.
Photograph by Jumping Rocks Photography

Facing Page Top: Visitors often wish to relax on the patio with a glass of wine, letting their worries disappear.
Photograph by Jumping Rocks Photography

Facing Page Bottom Left: The expansive front porch allows the relaxation and privacy that getaways promise.
Photograph by Jumping Rocks Photography

Facing Page Bottom Right: With a favorite book and a nap in mind, anyone can relax in one of the inn's Pawleys Island hammocks.
Photograph by Jumping Rocks Photography

Snowbird Mountain Lodge

Robbinsville, North Carolina

The nighttime view from the front porch of Snowbird Mountain Lodge is one of celestial grandeur. The absence of ambient light presents majestic star-field views as they appeared centuries ago, and only the placid sounds of nature abound at this remote mountain hideaway. Perched in the southern Appalachian Mountains in North Carolina, 25,000 acres of untouched forest blanket the horizon as far as the eye can see—and that is just the view from the front porch.

Originally built in 1940, Snowbird Mountain Lodge has not changed much since the lumber, stone and equipment used in its construction were carefully trucked up the mountain more than six decades ago. In 2004, the lodge was fully upgraded to current standard building codes and new building systems, while the existing architecture and interior spaces were carefully preserved, as the lodge is a part of both the National Register of Historic Places and National Trust for Historic Preservation.

Set in the middle of the Nantahala National Forest in the most remote county in the state of North Carolina, the serene backdrop for this quaint lodging is one that is often mistakenly thought to exist only in the American West. With more than a half-million acres under federal management, Nantahala is the largest of four national forests in the state, and its expansive terrain is home to an incomparable array of sublime natural features. Graham County, of which Robbinsville is a part, has more than 60,000 acres of lake water, including the 14,000-acre Lake Santeetlah just a few miles from Snowbird, providing convenient opportunities to enjoy the water via kayak, canoe, pontoon or power boat.

Top Left: Situated on the crest of a mountain, the lodge offers hospitality served Southern-style since 1941.
Photograph by Joyce Ardyn Durham

Bottom Left: Personal hot tubs let guests enjoy outstanding mountain vistas from the porch of the Chestnut Lodge while completely relaxing.
Photograph by Ron Johnson

Facing Page: The view from the lodge often reveals the reason behind the name Great Smoky Mountains.
Photograph by Joyce Ardyn Durham

America's most-rafted white-water river, the Nantahala River, is just 31 miles from the lodge and affords the prospect of an unmatched rafting experience. Within the broader setting of the Nantahala National Forest exists the Joyce Kilmer Memorial Forest, which is the largest stand of virgin hardwood timber east of the Rocky Mountains and extends ample hiking opportunities. The county is home to 197 miles of blue ribbon trout fishing, and Trout Unlimited's best native trout water in the South exists there as well. Once a day spent enjoying the unparalleled natural beauty of this exquisite, undisturbed landscape has concluded, guests return to the first-rate hospitality and splendor of Snowbird's delightful lodgings.

Snowbird's main lodge was originally completed in 1941 and is distinguished by its grand stone fireplace, cathedral ceiling and solid chestnut beams. Its 15 bedrooms are historically accurate, built period-specific to the 1940s and finished in distinctive native hardwoods. The rooms are all finished in wood that was actually saw-milled on site during the lodge's initial construction, and include such gracious woods as chestnut, wild cherry, silverbell and maple, among others. Outside the main lodge, the six-room chestnut lodge is comprised of distinctive rooms as well, forged from hemlock, hickory, oak, poplar, silverbell and maple. In-room amenities include fireplaces, king-sized beds, steam showers, hardwood floors, sitting areas, whirlpool tubs, a minibar, individual hot tubs and a private porch that overlooks the mountain. The more intimate Wolfe duplex cottage offers two similar rooms and is located at the edge of the forest. Its common front porch offers extraordinarily breathtaking mountain views and rockers for scenic leisure.

Above: The shining lights of Snowbird Mountain Lodge have been glowing brightly since 1941.
Photograph by Joyce Ardyn Durham

Facing Page Top: Rustic elegance can be found in the isolated Wolfe Cottage, where guests find traditional comfort and modern amenities.
Photograph by Joyce Ardyn Durham

Facing Page Bottom: The suites of Chestnut Lodge offer style, space and privacy that help visitors unwind and relax.
Photograph by Ron Johnson

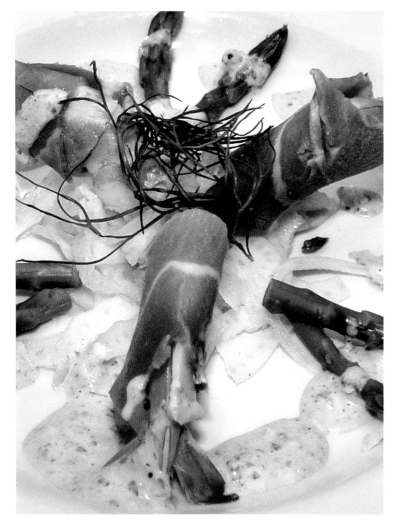

The main lodge also includes a 10,000-volume library, a wild cherry-paneled dining room and an outdoor dining terrace, both of which accommodate guests while they dine on Snowbird's cuisine. From sumptuous and unique breakfast offerings to gourmet picnic lunches to be enjoyed amidst the wondrous natural terrain, each dish is characterized by seasonal ingredients derived fresh from local streams and soil. The dinner menu includes enticing entrées such as stone-ground, cornmeal-crusted North Carolina mountain trout, hickory-smoked pork tenderloin with molasses barbecue jus and pesto-crusted salmon fillet, to name a few. The head chef responsible for these delectable culinary creations is none other than innkeeper Karen Rankin. In fact, in May 2000 the *Atlanta Journal-Constitution* wrote that Snowbird's cuisine was "as good as any Atlanta restaurant."

Above: The dining terrace offers openness and the sounds of nature throughout the changing seasons.
Photograph by Ron Johnson

Left: From the kitchen with love—Southern inspired gourmet meals have been featured in more than 10 national publications for their use of seasonal, local and fresh ingredients.
Photograph by Karen Rankin

Since 2004, the main lodge has included the well-stocked Fireside Bar, which includes 125 different beers—which are almost exclusively microbrews from across the United States—more than 300 bottles of liquor, more than 700 labels in its wine cellar and "the best selection of Scotch in the Southeast," Robert says. Live music is also a common scene at Snowbird, and the "house band," the Bluegrass Partners, performs 14 times annually at the lodge.

Whether seeking incomparable outdoor activities in a one-of-a-kind natural setting or simply looking to unplug from the hectic pace of modern life amidst a tranquil backdrop, Snowbird Mountain Lodge offers guests the opportunity to unwind in an amazing national forest environment that is second to none anywhere east of the Mississippi.

Above: There is no better way to unwind than in the Fireside Bar, featuring an outstanding selection with an award-winning wine list.
Photograph by Ron Johnson

Right: Readers can relax in comfort—day or evening—with one of more than 10,000 books in the lodge library.
Photograph by Joyce Ardyn Durham

The Swag Country Inn

Waynesville, North Carolina

When international travelers attending the 1982 Knoxville World's Fair needed lodging, Deener Matthews was asked to open her 250-acre estate for public accommodations. Built by Deener and her husband Dan in 1971 as a family retreat, this hand-hewn log, mountaintop lodge overlooks the Great Smoky Mountains, 12 miles outside of Waynesville, North Carolina. The original timber-beamed home held eight bedrooms and has grown to include 16 private rooms and cabins, housing up to 40 guests. Now in business for more than a quarter of a century, the inn's seven-month season runs from the early spring explosion of mountain wildflowers in late April to the photogenic colors of fall through Thanksgiving.

With personal touches from Deener, the inn offers old-fashioned hospitality with an attentive staff that is rare in today's busy world. A destination resort, The Swag includes all meals, plus the option of a gourmet brown bag lunch upon check-out with the celebrated Swag bar for dessert. Some favorite menu items include cider-simmered steel-cut Irish oats with plump raisins and apples for breakfast and a perfectly rich Roma tomato pie at the Wednesday gourmet picnic luncheon atop Gooseberry Knob. Tender venison, mountain trout, lollipop lamb chops and Angus filets are just some of the popular entrées accompanied by fresh herbs and vegetables from The Swag's own garden.

Situated atop a 5,000-foot mountain and nestled beside the border of the Great Smoky Mountains National Park, nature enthusiasts are guaranteed to fall in love with these ritzy rustic accommodations. Sharing a one-mile border with the park, The Swag has its own designated entrance. This places 500,000 acres of outdoor wilderness at the inn's back door for guests to enjoy. The local fauna include bear, wild turkey, owls, elk, red-tail hawks and even boar.

Top Left: Two guests' hiking sticks—with wooden medallion name tags—rest on the front porch after a leisurely walk in the Great Smoky Mountains National Park.
Photograph by Jumping Rocks Photography

Second Left: With a rolling wave of mountain peaks in the distance, The Swag house overlooks the American flag.
Photograph by John Warner

Third Left: The chef's venison entrée is garnished with fresh vegetables from The Swag's garden.
Photograph by Jumping Rocks Photography

Bottom Left: The gardener's scarecrow guards the organic herbs, flowers and a variety of vegetables.
Photograph by Jumping Rocks Photography

Facing Page: Two front-yard chairs await a peaceful moment, when the next guests will gaze at the early-morning fog in the valleys below.
Photograph by Jumping Rocks Photography

Housing one of the largest assemblies of species in the temperate world, the park monitors and protects around 100,000 different life forms that guests may observe. Many park naturalists study and document the Smoky Mountain life forms for a research initiative called All Taxa Biodiversity Inventory. This includes methods such as banding birds, while keeping track of their sex, age and health condition. For visitors who want an educational experience, guided hiking tours with supplemental slide shows are offered by some of the area's most qualified, knowledgeable personnel. Sitting on the Board of the Friends of the Smokies, Deener, too, is glad to share her knowledge of the area's wildlife.

With four mountain ranges visible from the inn, it is no wonder that outdoor activities abound. Guests who want to take a drive and explore sites off of the property can white-water raft, bike, horseback ride and golf. Also available on the property are wildflower workshops and hikes, horseshoes, croquet and badminton—all within viewing distance of the Plott Balsams, Richland Balsams and Black Mountains. For relaxing atop The Swag, there is an outdoor hot tub, and hammocks are sporadically nestled into secluded hideaways for romantic rests. Guests can also play racquetball in the regulation-size, underground, naturally cooled court.

Visitors are offered the opportunity to peek into unfamiliar lifestyles in the surrounding towns. The nearby Cherokee Indian reservation—45 minutes away—welcomes visitors, where indigenous cultures are displayed through an award-winning museum with crafts and artwork. For the ultimate extravagant architectural

Top Left: The private stone terrace opens out from the Terrace Bedroom with its rhododendron king-sized bed.
Photograph by Jumping Rocks Photography

Bottom Left: The master bedroom sits atop the Two Story, with a twig bed and spectacular view.
Photograph by Jumping Rocks Photography

Facing Page Top: The Swag living room is filled with comfortable tables and chairs and offers a large-paned window view of the mountain valleys below.
Photograph by Jumping Rocks Photography

Facing Page Bottom: During the hors d'oeuvres hour, The Swag dining room awaits its dinner guests. Seven o'clock is dinnertime, when guests feast upon the chef's four-course delights.
Photograph by Jumping Rocks Photography

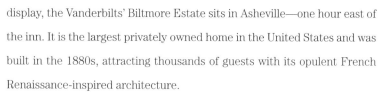

display, the Vanderbilts' Biltmore Estate sits in Asheville—one hour east of the inn. It is the largest privately owned home in the United States and was built in the 1880s, attracting thousands of guests with its opulent French Renaissance-inspired architecture.

The Swag's rustic, yet elegantly decorated rooms are a perfect retreat after a full day of exploring. Handmade quilts, early American antiques, woven rugs and Appalachian artifacts adorn the timber-beamed living room. The cozy 2,000-volume library lures guests to moments of quiet and literary reflection. Visitors can take advantage of the fresh coffee and tea assortment in their rooms, equipped with a bean grinder and brewer—the best way to start the day before putting a personalized walking stick to use. Ensuring that guests can stay in touch with the working world, the inn has XM Satellite Bose radio with wireless internet in each room and a *New York Times Digest* delivered to the guest's door each morning. An array of distinctly different rooms is offered, from the Two Story—with two separate bedrooms and a billiard room—to the Hideaway—a romantic

room of barn-siding, steam shower and large personal sauna for two. Other appealing amenities include private outdoor showers, idyllic secluded balconies, covered stone porches and large copper soaking tubs.

This award-winning mountaintop paradise is the ultimate in romantic high-country luxury. After more than 25 years, it continues to draw discriminating guests who yearn to have the busy world hushed and the fever of life removed.

Above Left: The whirlpool tub on the private balcony of the Two Story overlooks the distant Balsam Mountain range, which exceeds 6,000 feet.
Photograph by Jumping Rocks Photography

Above Right: The private porch off of Gail's Room faces the celebrated Cold Mountain, Mount Pisgah and, in the distance, the Asheville Valley.
Photograph by Jumping Rocks Photography

Facing Page: The living room of the Two Story lodging serves both the master bedroom upstairs and the main floor bedroom. The billiard room is on the lower level.
Photograph by Jumping Rocks Photography

Previous Page: The gazebo on Gooseberry Knob frames the mountains for The Swag's guests, ready to indulge in the Wednesday gourmet picnic—a few hundred yards from The Swag house. The gazebo sits near the boundary of the Great Smoky Mountains National Park.
Photograph by Jumping Rocks Photography

Two Meeting Street Inn

Charleston, South Carolina

No other place is like Charleston, and in Charleston, no place is quite like Two Meeting Street Inn—the jewel in the crown of the city's bed-and-breakfasts. From historic Two Meeting Street Inn's gracious southern veranda—one of the most photographed porches in the South—guests enjoy layer upon layer of natural beauty while perusing literature or indulging in afternoon tea with an enticing array of lemon squares, rum cakes, plantation brownies, crackers and savory spreads. Immediately surrounded by century-old live oaks amid lush gardens with a closely clipped lawn and familiarly exotic blooms that represent formal perfection, the inn overlooks Charleston's historic harbor, tip of the Battery and White Point Gardens; a few blocks away, world-class dining, modern boutiques, antique shops, art galleries, historic museum houses and cultural festivals await. Outside and in, the regal post-bellum Queen Anne Victorian lives up to its reputation as the grand dame of Charleston's historic inns.

Emanating a rare charm, as the city's oldest inn and one of few that share its caliber, Two Meeting Street welcomes guests with its bright façade, dramatic turrets, profusion of arched columns and nine stained glass windows—it makes a memorable impression. The stately inn's broad, sweeping curves beckon all to enter. The foyer establishes much of the house's character through a generous use of finely grained English oak, a massive staircase that climbs in three stages to the second floor and a large mantel with mirrored pediment. Museum-quality antiques, period-inspired furnishings and other family heirlooms create an overwhelming sense of warmth and comfort.

Top Left: The Williams Room—one of the inn's premier Victorian rooms—features a working fireplace and a private second-floor balcony that overlooks the courtyard.
Photograph courtesy of Two Meeting Street Inn

Second Left: The veranda provides an ideal setting for relaxing and enjoying the property while viewing the lush garden and Charleston's historic harbor beyond Battery Park.
Photograph courtesy of Two Meeting Street Inn

Third Left: Fine English hand-carved oak and a sunburst stained glass window enrich the dining room where guests enjoy breakfast and afternoon tea.
Photograph courtesy of Two Meeting Street Inn

Bottom Left: The legendary Tiffany stained glass windows were installed by Louis Comfort Tiffany in 1895; a painting of the current owner on her wedding day hangs adjacent.
Photograph courtesy of Two Meeting Street Inn

Facing Page: Built in 1890, the inn reigns as a graceful masterpiece of Queen Anne architecture with softly rounded lines and two tiers of verandas.
Photograph courtesy of Two Meeting Street Inn

Two Meeting Street exudes the gentility of a bygone era, and rightly so as it was built in 1890 with the $75,000 that George Walton Williams, a highly successful merchant, gifted his daughter Martha upon her betrothal to Waring P. Carrington, a respected jeweler. Customary for the times, the couple chose a site near the Williams' residence—the renowned Calhoun Mansion—to place their first home. Two of the nine distinctively designed rooms are named after these families; a third, after the Spell family, which has lovingly cared for the estate since the 1940s. A decade prior, the Carringtons' daughter Sallie subtly evolved the estate into a guesthouse as a way to maintain the family treasure. All who have lived and served at Two Meeting Street, from the original owners to the three generations of Spells, have been congenial Southern hosts.

Each room unfolds into the next, and the fluidity is especially noticeable as guests make their way through common areas such as the enchanting, oval-shaped dining room. Guests enjoy the entire house, but there is something about the sweeping, double-tiered, arched verandas with lush plants, slow-moving ceiling fans, Southern rockers and wicker furniture that draws guests to this special location. From this vantage point, guests watch the world go by. Outside the gate is perpetual motion—joggers, walkers of dogs, visitors in horse-drawn carriages with drivers who quote the history of the house, a wedding in the park, ships afloat and birds aloft over the harbor. Within the gates, the house and grounds become a sanctuary.

Two Meeting Street is counted among 1,000 places people should visit in their lifetime, and while any area of the inn is worthy of such praise, the parlor is perhaps the most deserving, as it possesses two Tiffany stained glass windows, which were presented to Martha Carrington on her fifth wedding anniversary—the installation was personally overseen by Louis Comfort Tiffany. Tiffany's magic in color and design makes nature come alive in the Southern fauna of iris, magnolia and dogwood. Carefully designed, executed and preserved details such as this comprise the refined tapestry of Two Meeting Street Inn—a place of elegance coupled with comfort. Its genuine character and unmatched ambience have led guests to proclaim: "Never have we stayed in a place so beautiful or so lovingly cared for, nor have we ever felt as pampered."

Right: The English oak foyer and grand staircase graciously welcome guests to the splendor of a well-to-do Victorian past. The original Czechoslovakian crystal chandelier is stunning.
Photograph courtesy of Two Meeting Street Inn

Facing Page Top: The Queen Anne Room is a large, oval-shaped Victorian room on the second floor with 12-foot ceilings, hardwood flooring and an original turn-of-the-century bathroom.
Photograph courtesy of Two Meeting Street Inn

Facing Page Bottom: Guests enjoy afternoon tea or breakfast on the wraparound piazza while gazing at century-old live oak trees in the garden, enjoying the harbor breeze and watching sailing ships pass.
Photograph courtesy of Two Meeting Street Inn

Featured Inns of Select Registry

1842 Inn
Macon, Georgia

1889 WhiteGate Inn & Cottage
Asheville, North Carolina

1906 Pine Crest Inn & Restaurant
Tryon, North Carolina

Abigail's Hotel
Victoria, British Columbia

Abingdon Manor
Latta, South Carolina

Adair Country Inn and Restaurant
Bethlehem, New Hampshire

Adele Turner Inn
Newport, Rhode Island

The Aerie Bed & Breakfast
New Bern, North Carolina

Albemarle Inn
Asheville, North Carolina

Albergo Allegria
Windham, New York

Allaire Timbers Inn
Breckenridge, Colorado

The Amelia Island Williams House
Fernandina Beach, Florida

Amethyst Inn at Regents Park
Victoria, British Columbia

Antietam Overlook Farm
Keedysville, Maryland

Antrim 1844 Country Inn
Taneytown, Maryland

Applegate Inn
Lee, Massachusetts

Applewood Inn
Guerneville, California

Arrowhead Inn
Durham, North Carolina

Arsenic and Old Lace Bed & Breakfast Inn
Eureka Springs, Arkansas

Asa Ransom House
Clarence, New York

The Ashby Inn & Restaurant
Paris, Virginia

Auberge des Gallant
Saint Marthe-Rigaud, Quebec

Auberge Lakeview Inn
Lac-Brome City, Knowlton, Quebec

Auberge Roche des Brises
St-Joseph-du-Lac, Quebec

Aurora Inn and E.B. Morgan House
Aurora, New York

Baladerry Inn at Gettysburg
Gettysburg, Pennsylvania

The Ballard Inn & Restaurant
Ballard, California

The Ballastone Inn
Savannah, Georgia

Barley Sheaf Farm Estate & Spa
Holicong, Pennsylvania

Barrows House
Dorset, Vermont

Beach Bed & Breakfast
St. Simons Island, Georgia

Beaconsfield Inn
Victoria, British Columbia

A Beckmann Inn & Carriage House
San Antonio, Texas

Bed & Breakfast Inn at La Jolla
La Jolla, California

Beechmont Bed and Breakfast Inn
Hanover, Pennsylvania

Beechwood Inn
Clayton, Georgia

The Bellmoor
Rehoboth Beach, Delaware

Berry Manor Inn
Rockland, Maine

Berry Springs Lodge
Sevierville, Tennessee

Birchwood Inn
Lenox, Massachusetts

Bissell House Bed & Breakfast Inn
South Pasadena, California

Black Walnut Bed & Breakfast Inn
Asheville, North Carolina

Blacksmith Inn On the Shore
Baileys Harbor, Wisconsin

Blair Hill Inn at Moosehead Lake
Greenville, Maine

Blair House
Wimberley, Texas

The Blue Hill Inn
Blue Hill, Maine

Bonne Terre Country Inn & Restaurant
Nesbit, Mississippi

The Boothby Inn
Erie, Pennsylvania

Brampton Inn
Chestertown, Maryland

The Brentwood, A Bed and Breakfast
Brentwood, Tennessee

The Briars
Jackson's Point, Ontario

Brierley Hill Bed & Breakfast
Lexington, Virginia

Brightwood Inn
Oglesby, Illinois

Brook Farm Inn
Lenox, Massachusetts

Buhl Mansion Guesthouse & Spa
Sharon, Pennsylvania

Burlington's Willis Graves Bed and Breakfast Inn
Burlington, Kentucky

The Buttonwood Inn
North Conway, New Hampshire

Camden Maine Stay
Camden, Maine

Cameron Estate Inn & Restaurant
Mount Joy, Pennsylvania

The Campbell House, A City Inn
Eugene, Oregon

Candlelight Inn
North Wildwood, New Jersey

Canyon Villa Inn
Sedona, Arizona

The Captain Freeman Inn
Brewster, Cape Cod, Massachusetts

Captain Lindsey House Inn
Rockland, Maine

The Captain Lord Mansion
Kennebunkport, Maine

Captain's House Inn
Chatham, Massachusetts

Carpe Diem Guesthouse
Provincetown, Massachusetts

Carter House Inns
Eureka, California

Casa de las Chimeneas
Taos, New Mexico

Casa Laguna Inn & Spa
Laguna Beach, California

Casa Sedona Bed & Breakfast Inn
Sedona, Arizona

Castle Marne
Denver, Colorado

Cathedral Mountain Lodge
Field, British Columbia

Central Park Bed & Breakfast
Louisville, Kentucky

Channel House Inn
Depoe Bay, Oregon

Chanticleer Inn
Lookout Mountain, Georgia

The Charles Street Inn
Boston, Massachusetts

Chesterfield Inn
Chesterfield, New Hampshire

Chestnut Inn
Deposit, New York

Chimney Hill Farm Estate
Lambertville, New Jersey

Christmas Farm Inn and Spa
Jackson, New Hampshire

Christopher Place
Newport, Tennessee

Chrysalis Inn and Spa
Bellingham, Washington

Cliffside Inn
Newport, Rhode Island

Colby Hill Inn
Henniker, New Hampshire

Colette's Bed and Breakfast
Port Angeles, Washington

Coombs Inn
Apalachicola, Florida

The Copper Beech Inn
Ivoryton, Connecticut

Crestmont Inn
Eagles Mere, Pennsylvania

Crisanver House
Shrewsbury, Vermont

Crowne Pointe Historic Inn
Provincetown, Massachusetts

The Cypress Inn
Conway, South Carolina

The Dan'l Webster Inn and Spa
Sandwich, Massachusetts

The Darby Field Inn
Albany, New Hampshire

Deerfield Inn
Deerfield, Massachusetts

Deerhill Inn
West Dover, Vermont

Deerpark Country Inn
Buckhannon, West Virginia

Devonfield Inn
Lee, Massachusetts

Dockside Guest Quarters
York, Maine

The Domain of Killien
Haliburton, Ontario

The Duke Mansion
Charlotte, North Carolina

The Dunbar House, 1880
Murphys, California

Durlacher Hof Alpine Inn
Whistler, British Columbia

Eagles Mere Inn
Eagles Mere, Pennsylvania

Eastman Inn
North Conway, New Hampshire

Eight Gables Inn
Gatlinburg, Tennessee

El Farolito Bed & Breakfast Inn and Four Kachinas Inn
Santa Fe, New Mexico

Elizabeth Pointe Lodge
Amelia Island, Florida

Emerson Inn by the Sea
Rockport, Massachusetts

Emma Nevada House
Nevada City, California

The Empress of Little Rock
Little Rock, Arkansas

The English Inn
Eaton Rapids, Michigan

The Fairbanks House
Amelia Island, Florida

Fairthorne Cottage Bed & Breakfast
Cape May, New Jersey

Fairview Inn
Jackson, Mississippi

Fairville Inn
Chadds Ford, Pennsylvania

Fall Farm, A Fine Country Inn
Mineola, Texas

Foley House Inn
Savannah, Georgia

Fort Lewis Lodge
Millboro, Virginia

The Four Columns Inn
Newfane, Vermont

Fox Creek Inn
Chittenden, Vermont

Fox 'n' Hound Bed and Breakfast
Saratoga Springs, New York

Frederick House
Staunton, Virginia

French Manor
South Sterling, Pennsylvania

Friends Lake Inn
Chestertown, New York

Gaige House, A Thompson Hotel
Glen Ellen, California

Gallatin River Lodge
Bozeman, Montana

Garth Woodside Mansion
Hannibal, Missouri

Gateway Lodge Country Inn
Cooksburg, Pennsylvania

Gateways Inn
Lenox, Massachusetts

Genesee Country Inn Bed & Breakfast
Mumford, New York

Geneva on the Lake
Geneva, New York

Gerstle Park Inn
San Rafael, California

Gideon Ridge Inn
Blowing Rock, North Carolina

Gingerbread Mansion Inn
Ferndale, California

Glasbern
Fogelsville, Pennsylvania

Glendeven Inn
Mendocino, California

Glen-Ella Springs
Clarkesville, Georgia

Glenlaurel–A Scottish Country Inn
Rockbridge, Ohio

The Glynn House Inn
Ashland, New Hampshire

Goldmoor Inn
Galena, Illinois

Governor's House Inn
Charleston, South Carolina

The Governor's Inn
Ludlow, Vermont

Grape Leaf Inn
Healdsburg, California

Graystone Inn
Wilmington, North Carolina

Great Oak Manor Inn
Chestertown, Maryland

Greyfield Inn
Cumberland Island, Georgia

The Greystone Inn
Lake Toxaway, North Carolina

The Griswold Inn
Essex, Connecticut

The Groveland Hotel
Groveland, California

Hacienda del Sol
Taos, New Mexico

Haddonfield Inn
Haddonfield, New Jersey

The Halliburton
Halifax, Nova Scotia

Hamanassett Bed & Breakfast
Chadds Ford, Pennsylvania

Hamilton-Turner Inn
Savannah, Georgia

The Hancock Inn
Hancock, New Hampshire

Harbor House Inn by the Sea
Elk, California

Harbor Light Inn
Marblehead, Massachusetts

Harbour House
Niagara-on-the-Lake, Ontario

Hartstone Inn
Camden, Maine

Hartwell House Inn
Ogunquit, Maine

Haven By The Sea
Wells Beach, Maine

Hawthorne Inn
Concord, Massachusetts

Heart of the Village Inn
Shelburne, Vermont

Henderson Village
Perry, Georgia

Hermann Hill Vineyard & Inn
Hermann, Missouri

Heron House
Key West, Florida

The Herr Tavern & Publick House
Gettysburg, Pennsylvania

Hickory Bridge Farm
Orrtanna, Pennsylvania

A Hidden Haven
Port Angeles, Washington

Historic Jacob Hill Inn
Providence, Rhode Island

Hobbit Hollow Farm
Skaneateles, New York

The Honor Mansion
Healdsburg, California

House on Bayou Road
New Orleans, Louisiana

The Humphrey Hughes House
Cape May, New Jersey

Hydrangea House Inn
Newport, Rhode Island

The Inn Above Onion Creek
Kyle, Texas

The Inn and Spa at Cedar Falls
Logan, Ohio

The Inn and Spa at Intercourse Village
Intercourse, Pennsylvania

The Inn at Bay Ledge
Bar Harbor, Maine

The Inn at Black Star Farms
Suttons Bay, Michigan

The Inn at Bowman's Hill
New Hope, Pennsylvania

The Inn at Cooperstown
Cooperstown, New York

Inn at Crotched Mountain
Francestown, New Hampshire

Inn at Dresden
Dresden, Ohio

The Inn at El Gaucho
Seattle, Washington

The Inn at Honey Run
Millersburg, Ohio

Inn at Iris Meadows
Waynesville, North Carolina

The Inn at Millrace Pond
Hope, New Jersey

Inn at Montchanin Village
Wilmington, Delaware

Inn at New Berlin
New Berlin, Pennsylvania

The Inn at Oak Street
Jacksonville, Florida

The Inn at Occidental
Occidental, California

Inn at Ormsby Hill
Manchester, Vermont

Inn at Richmond
Richmond, Massachusetts

Inn at Riverbend
Pearisburg, Virginia

The Inn at Round Barn Farm
Waitsfield, Vermont

Inn at Sawmill Farm
West Dover, Vermont

The Inn at Stockbridge
Stockbridge, Massachusetts

Inn at Stonington
Stonington, Connecticut

The Inn at Sunrise Point
Camden, Maine

Inn at Thorn Hill
Jackson, New Hampshire

The Inn at Turkey Hill
Bloomsburg, Pennsylvania

Inn at Vaucluse Spring
Stephens City, Virginia

Inn at Warner Hall
Gloucester, Virginia

Inn at Water's Edge
Ludlow, Vermont

The Inn by the Bandstand
Exeter, New Hampshire

Inn on Church Street
Hendersonville, North Carolina

Inn on Lake Granbury
Granbury, Texas

The Inn on Negley
Pittsburgh, Pennsylvania

Inn on Oak Creek
Sedona, Arizona

Inn on the Common
Craftsbury Common, Vermont

Inn on the Twenty
Jordan, Ontario

Inne at Watson's Choice and
Harvest House Bed & Breakfast
Uniontown, Pennsylvania

Inns At Blackberry Common
Camden, Maine

Isaiah Jones Homestead
Sandwich, Massachusetts

J. Patrick House Bed & Breakfast Inn
Cambria, California

Jacksonville Inn
Jacksonville, Oregon

Jakobstettel Inn
St. Jacobs, Ontario

John Rutledge House Inn
Charleston, South Carolina

Jordan Hollow Farm Inn
Stanley, Virginia

Joshua Grindle Inn
Mendocino, California

Joshua Wilton House Inn
Harrisonburg, Virginia

Juniper Hill Inn
Windsor, Vermont

Kehoe House
Savannah, Georgia

Kensington Riverside Inn
Calgary, Alberta

The King's Cottage
Lancaster, Pennsylvania

La Farge Perry House
Newport, Rhode Island

La Zarzuela, A B&B Inn
Tucson, Arizona

The Lafayette Inn
Easton, Pennsylvania

Lake Pointe Inn
McHenry, Maryland

Lang House on Main Street
Burlington, Vermont

L'Auberge Provençale
White Post, Virginia

Le Domaine
Hancock, Maine

The Lodge at Moosehead Lake
Greenville, Maine

Lodge at Sedona
Sedona, Arizona

Lodge on Gorhams Bluff
Pisgah, Alabama

The Lodge on Lake Lure
Lake Lure, North Carolina

Lodge on Little St. Simons Island
Little St. Simons Island, Georgia

Long Beach Lodge Resort
Tofino, British Columbia

Lookout Point Lakeside Inn
Hot Springs, Arkansas

The Lords Proprietors' Inn
Edenton, North Carolina

Los Poblanos Inn
Albuquerque, New Mexico

Maine Stay Inn & Cottages
Kennebunkport, Maine

The Mainstay Inn
Cape May, New Jersey

Manor House Inn
Bar Harbor, Maine

Manor House
Norfolk, Connecticut

Manor on Golden Pond
Holderness, New Hampshire

Mansion Hill Inn
Madison, Wisconsin

The Maple Leaf Inn
Barnard, Vermont

Market Street Inn
Taylorville, Illinois

Marquesa Hotel
Key West, Florida

Martine Inn
Pacific Grove, California

The Mast Farm Inn
Valle Crucis, North Carolina

Mayor's Mansion Inn
Chattanooga, Tennessee

McCaffrey House Bed & Breakfast Inn
Twain Harte, California

Mercersburg Inn
Mercersburg, Pennsylvania

Middleton Inn
Washington, Virginia

Mill House Inn
East Hampton, New York

Mill Rose Inn
Half Moon Bay, California

The Millcroft Inn and Spa
Village of Alton-Caledon, Ontario

Monmouth Plantation
Natchez, Mississippi

The Monteagle Inn
Monteagle, Tennessee

Montford Inn and Cottages
Norman, Oklahoma

Montrose Hideaway B&B Retreat
Daphne, Alabama

The Morehead Inn
Charlotte, North Carolina

Morgan-Samuels Inn
Canandaigua, New York

Murphin Ridge Inn
West Union, Ohio

National House Inn
Marshall, Michigan

Noble Inns
San Antonio, Texas

Normandy Inn
Spring Lake, New Jersey

North Fork Mountain Inn
Smoke Hole, West Virginia

Notchland Inn
Hart's Location, New Hampshire

The Oaks Victorian Inn
Christiansburg, Virginia

October Country Inn
Bridgewater Corners, Vermont

The Ogé House on the Riverwalk
San Antonio, Texas

Old Fort Inn
Kennebunkport, Maine

The Old Harbor Inn
Chatham, Massachusetts

Old Monterey Inn
Monterey, California

Old Rittenhouse Inn
Bayfield, Wisconsin

Old Town Guest House
Colorado Springs, Colorado

The Oliver Inn
South Bend, Indiana

Orchard Hill Country Inn
Julian, California

The Orchard Inn
Saluda, North Carolina

Packwood House
Skaneateles, New York

Palmer House Inn
Falmouth, Massachusetts

Pearson's Pond Luxury Inn
Juneau, Alaska

Penny House Inn
Eastham, Massachusetts

Pentagöet Inn
Castine, Maine

Pilgrim's Inn
Deer Isle, Maine

Pomegranate Inn
Portland, Maine

Portland's White House Bed & Breakfast
Portland, Oregon

Prospect Hill Plantation Inn
Charlottesville, Virginia

The Queen Victoria
Cape May, New Jersey

Rabbit Hill Inn
Lower Waterford, Vermont

Reynolds Mansion
Bellefonte, Pennsylvania

The Rhett House Inn
Beaufort, South Carolina

Richmond Hill Inn
Asheville, North Carolina

Richmont Inn
Townsend, Tennessee

Ripplecove Inn
Ayer's Cliff, Quebec

The Robert Morris Inn
Oxford, Maryland

Romantic RiverSong Inn
Estes Park, Colorado

Rose Hill Inn
Marshall, Michigan

Rose Hill Manor
Stonewall, Texas

The Sand Castle
Long Beach Island, New Jersey

The Sanford House Inn & Spa
Arlington, Texas

Santa Ynez Inn
Santa Ynez, California

The Sayre Mansion
Bethlehem, Pennsylvania

Sea Rock Inn
Mendocino, California

The Settlers Inn
Hawley, Pennsylvania

Seven Sea Street Inn
Nantucket, Massachusetts

Shaw's Restaurant & Inn
Lancaster, Ohio

The Shelburne Inn
Seaview, Washington

The Shellmont Inn
Atlanta, Georgia

Sheppard Mansion
Hanover, Pennsylvania

The Sherwood Inn
Skaneateles, New York

Shiloh Morning Inn and Cottages
Ardmore, Oklahoma

Shipwright Inn
Charlottetown, Prince Edward Island

Shore House at Lake Tahoe
Tahoe Vista, California

Silver Thatch Inn
Charlottesville, Virginia

Simpson House Inn
Santa Barbara, California

The Skelton House
Hartwell, Georgia

Snowbird Mountain Lodge
Robbinsville, North Carolina

Sooke Harbour House
Sooke, British Columbia

Southmoreland on the Plaza
Kansas City, Missouri

Spencer House Inn Bed & Breakfast
St. Marys, Georgia

The Squire Tarbox Inn
Westport Island, Maine

St. Francis Inn
St. Augustine, Florida

Stafford's Bay View Inn
Petoskey, Michigan

Stewart Inn Bed and Breakfast
Wausau, Wisconsin

Stone Hill Inn
Stowe, Vermont

Stonecroft Country Inn
Ledyard, Connecticut

Stoney Creek Farm
Boonsboro, Maryland

A Storybook Inn
Versailles, Kentucky

Sugar Hill Inn
Franconia, New Hampshire

Sugar Tree Inn
Steeles Tavern, Virginia

The Swag Country Inn
Waynesville, North Carolina

Swann House
Washington, D.C.

Swift House Inn
Middlebury, Vermont

Swiss Woods
Lititz, Pennsylvania

Tanque Verde Ranch
Tucson, Arizona

Tara–A Country Inn
Clark, Pennsylvania

Taughannock Farms Inn
Trumansburg, New York

Thomas Shepherd Inn
Shepherdstown, West Virginia

Thorncroft Inn
Martha's Vineyard, Massachusetts

Three Mountain Inn
Jamaica, Vermont

Turtleback Farm Inn
Eastsound, Washington

Two Meeting Street Inn
Charleston, South Carolina

Ullikana and Yellow House
Bar Harbor, Maine

Union Street Inn
Nantucket, Massachusetts

Vendue Inn
Charleston, South Carolina

The Verandas
Wilmington, North Carolina

Victoria House
Spring Lake, New Jersey

Victorian Treasure Inn
Lodi, Wisconsin

Victoria's Historic Inn & Carriage House
Wolfville, Nova Scotia

Villa Marco Polo Inn
Victoria, British Columbia

Villa Royale Inn
Palm Springs, California

The Washington House Inn
Cedarburg, Wisconsin

Washington Square Inn
San Francisco, California

The Waterford Inne
Waterford, Maine

The Waverly Inn
Hendersonville, North Carolina

Weasku Inn
Grants Pass, Oregon

The Weathervane Inn
South Egremont, Massachusetts

Wedmore Place
Williamsburg, Virginia

West End Inn
Portland, Maine

West Mountain Inn
Arlington, Vermont

The Westchester House
Saratoga Springs, New York

The Whalewalk Inn
Eastham, Massachusetts

Whispering Pines Bed & Breakfast
Dellroy, Ohio

Whistling Swan Inn
Stanhope, New Jersey

The White Doe Inn
Manteo, North Carolina

The White Gull Inn
Fish Creek, Wisconsin

White Lace Inn
Sturgeon Bay, Wisconsin

White Oak Inn
Danville, Ohio

Whitestone Country Inn
Kingston, Tennessee

Wickwood Inn
Saugatuck, Michigan

The Wild Iris Inn
LaConner, Washington

WildSpring Guest Habitat
Port Orford, Oregon

Willard Street Inn
Burlington, Vermont

Willcox House Country Inn
Seabeck, Washington

The Willcox
Aiken, South Carolina

The William Henry Miller Inn
Ithaca, New York

The William Seward Inn
Westfield, New York

Windemere Inn By The Sea
Indialantic, Florida

Windham Hill Inn
West Townshend, Vermont

Wine Country Inn
St. Helena, California

The Wooden Duck
Newton, New Jersey

Woolverton Inn
Stockton, New Jersey

Yates House Bed and Breakfast
Rocheport, Missouri

The Yellow House
Waynesville, North Carolina

Publishing Team

PUBLISHER: Brian G. Carabet

PUBLISHER: John A. Shand

EXECUTIVE PUBLISHER: Phil Reavis

DIRECTOR OF DEVELOPMENT & DESIGN: Beth Benton

DIRECTOR OF BOOK MARKETING & DISTRIBUTION: Julia Hoover

PUBLICATION MANAGER: Lauren B. Castelli

SENIOR GRAPHIC DESIGNER: Emily Kattan

GRAPHIC DESIGNER: Jonathan Fehr

GRAPHIC DESIGNER: Ashley Rodges

GRAPHIC DESIGNER: Red Scofield

EDITORIAL DEVELOPMENT SPECIALIST: Elizabeth Gionta

MANAGING EDITOR: Rosalie Z. Wilson

EDITOR: Katrina Autem

EDITOR: Amanda Bray

EDITOR: Anita M. Kasmar

EDITOR: Ryan Parr

EDITOR: Daniel Reid

MANAGING PRODUCTION COORDINATOR: Kristy Randall

PRODUCTION COORDINATOR: Laura K. Greenwood

PRODUCTION COORDINATOR: Jennifer Lenhart

TRAFFIC COORDINATOR: Amanda Johnson

ADMINISTRATIVE MANAGER: Carol Kendall

ADMINISTRATIVE ASSISTANT: Beverly Smith

CLIENT SUPPORT COORDINATOR: Amanda Mathers

CLIENT SUPPORT ASSISTANT: Meghan Anderson

PANACHE PARTNERS, LLC
CORPORATE HEADQUARTERS
1424 Gables Court
Plano, TX 75075
469.246.6060
www.panache.com

Above: Kensington Riverside Inn, page 24

THE PANACHE COLLECTION

Dream Homes Series

Dream Homes of Texas
Dream Homes South Florida
Dream Homes Colorado
Dream Homes Metro New York
Dream Homes Greater Philadelphia
Dream Homes New Jersey
Dream Homes Florida
Dream Homes Southwest
Dream Homes Northern California
Dream Homes Carolinas
Dream Homes Chicago
Dream Homes Georgia
Dream Homes Pacific Northwest
Dream Homes Deserts
Dream Homes Greater Washington, D.C.
Dream Homes Minnesota
Dream Homes Los Angeles
Dream Homes Coastal California
Dream Homes New England
Dream Homes Michigan
Dream Homes Tennessee
Dream Homes Ohio & Pennsylvania
Dream Homes London

Additional Titles

Spectacular Hotels
Spectacular Golf of Texas
Spectacular Golf of Colorado
Spectacular Restaurants of Texas
Extraordinary Homes California
Spectacular Wineries of Napa Valley
Spectacular Wineries of New York
Spectacular Wineries of Sonoma
Spectacular Wineries of Coastal California
Art of Celebration: New York Style
Visions of Design
Distinguished Inns of North America

City by Design Series

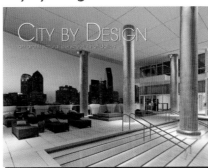

City by Design Dallas
City by Design Atlanta
City by Design San Francisco
City by Design Chicago
City by Design Charlotte
City by Design Phoenix, Tucson & Albuquerque
City by Design Denver
City by Design Orlando
City by Design Austin, Houston & San Antonio
City by Design Washington, D.C.

Perspectives on Design Series

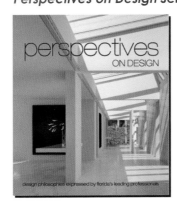

Perspectives on Design Florida
Perspectives on Design Dallas
Perspectives on Design New England
Perspectives on Design Pacific Northwest

Spectacular Homes Series

Spectacular Homes of Texas
Spectacular Homes of Georgia
Spectacular Homes of South Florida
Spectacular Homes of Tennessee
Spectacular Homes of the Pacific Northwest
Spectacular Homes of Greater Philadelphia
Spectacular Homes of the Southwest
Spectacular Homes of Colorado
Spectacular Homes of the Carolinas
Spectacular Homes of Florida
Spectacular Homes of California
Spectacular Homes of Michigan
Spectacular Homes of the Heartland
Spectacular Homes of Chicago
Spectacular Homes of Washington, D.C.
Spectacular Homes of Ohio & Pennsylvania
Spectacular Homes of Minnesota
Spectacular Homes of New England
Spectacular Homes of New York
Spectacular Homes of Western Canada
Spectacular Homes of Toronto
Spectacular Homes of London

Visit www.panache.com
or call 469.246.6060

PANACHE PARTNERS, LLC

Creating Spectacular Publications
for Discerning Readers

Above: Wine Country Inn, page 44